One Moment Can Change a Soul

One Moment Can Change a Soul

Helping Catholics Come Home

Tom Peterson

FOREWORD BY SCOTT HAHN

Our Sunday Visitor
Huntington, Indiana

Our Sunday Visitor Publishing Division
Our Sunday Visitor, Inc.
200 Noll Plaza
Huntington, IN 46750
www.osv.com
1-800-348-2440

ISBN: 978-1-68192-584-4 (Inventory No. T2453)
1. RELIGION—Christian Life—Personal Growth.
2. RELIGION—Christian Life—Inspirational.
3. RELIGION—Christianity—Catholic.

eISBN: 978-1-68192-585-1
LCCN: 2020932450

Cover and interior design: Lindsey Riesen
Cover art: Adobe Stock

Printed in the United States of America

This book is a second and enhanced edition of *Catholics Come Home: God's Extraordinary Plan for Your Life*, published by Penguin Random House. It has been significantly revised and updated, with a new title. Our prayerful hope is that more faithful, practicing Catholics like you will be inspired by this book to more actively share your gift of faith with others, and thereby help Jesus bring more souls to heaven.

This book is dedicated to my wife, Tricia; my daughters Katie, Kimberly, and Kristina; sons-in-law Raymond and Brian; and grandchildren RJ, Hannah, Savannah, Dominic, and Lily (and those who follow). May you always be thankful for the gift of your Catholic Faith in Christ, and share this amazing gift with the whole world.

Contents

Contents

Foreword

Dr. Scott Hahn

We are in the midst of a New Evangelization; and I believe this book is a signal moment in its success. This book is a grace from God. It is also a sign that will lead many folks back home to the family of God, which is the Catholic Church.

Perhaps it would be good to explain what is meant by the New Evangelization? After all, Catholics have been hearing about it for the last few decades. During the pontificate of Pope Saint John Paul II, we heard of it often. It was something he saw very clearly, as if on the horizon. It's a destination toward which he patiently moved us. Way back in 1979, near the beginning of his reign as pope, he mentioned it in passing when he spoke at Nowa Huta, Poland, which was then a communist "worker's paradise" and is now a Christian pilgrimage destination (because John Paul II preached there). In 1983 he spoke of the New Evangelization for the first time in a focused, intentional way, and it was already programmatic. It defined a vision. He said, while speaking to the bishops of Latin America, that the New Evangelization was to be officially launched in 1992, because that would mark the five hundredth anniversary of the founding and first evangelizing of the Americas.

Think about it: In 1492, the three most populous Catholic countries were Spain, Italy, and France. Fast-forward five hundred years, and the three most populous Catholic countries on earth today are Brazil, Mexico, and the United States, countries that did not even exist in 1492. As Europe used to be the world's center, so now it is the Americas. And what will be in five hundred years may well depend on how we respond to the urgent call of Christ's vicars to the task of the New Evangelization. In retrospect, we can see why John Paul II looked back — and forward — to a New Evangelization that would begin in the Americas.

In preparation for that launch, he published an encyclical in 1990, *Redemptoris Missio*, and there he stated: "I sense that the moment has come to commit all of the Church's energies to a new evangelization. ... No believer in Christ, no institution of the Church can avoid this supreme duty: to proclaim Christ to all peoples."

John Paul II went on to describe the decade of the 1990s as an extended "Advent season" for the New Evangelization. In short, as Advent marks the start of a new liturgical year, so the last decade of the twentieth century marked the beginning of the New Evangelization. This was clearly never intended to be a short-term campaign. It was a priority for John Paul II from the early years of his pontificate, and he carried the New Evangelization into the new millennium. Likewise, Pope Benedict renewed the call with even greater emphasis, and made it clear that it is to continue for the rest of the twenty-first century!

Indeed, if some people thought of the New Evangelization as John Paul II's private catchphrase, they have by now been completely disabused of that notion. Not only did Pope Benedict take it up with gusto, but Pope Francis has also used it.

Pope Benedict specified more precisely what it means. In his teaching, he referred to two distinct "branches" of evangelization: On the one hand, "evangelization" refers to the continuous practice of the Church's missionaries who have always gone out to proclaim the Gospel to those who have never heard of Jesus Christ and his message of salvation. On the other hand, he clarified that "the New Evangelization is directed principally at those who, though baptized, have drifted away from the Church and live without reference to the Christian life."

In other words, Pope Benedict asked all of us to take up the work that Catholics Come Home® has been doing now for years

— the very task that's set before us in this book. Yes, we need to reach those millions who have never heard of Christ; but first and foremost, we need to dedicate ourselves to evangelizing the baptized — to reaching those prodigal sons and daughters who have strayed from the Church. They're outside the Church looking at its stained-glass windows, which look pretty drab from the street. But if we get these people to come back inside, they'll see — and remember — the glorious, luminous beauty when the light shines in from above.

The Church "exists," said Pope Saint Paul VI, "in order to evangelize." It is the work not just of foreign missionaries, but also of the whole Church. Evangelization is what we do — because we're Christian, because we're Catholic. More than that, it's who we are. If we don't evangelize, we simply do not exist as Christians. Isn't it tragic that we can speak today of so many "formerly Christian" lands, in the Middle East, in Europe … in the Americas?

We will be patient, as the popes have been, but we must not be slack. We must feel the urgency of the sacred authors who cried out "How long?" (Ps 6:3) even as they knew that their Redeemer lives (see Jb 19:25) and that everything would work together for the good (Rom 8:28).

We do need to re-evangelize countries that have been de-Christianized, beginning with our own. It is sad that we can speak of many once-Christian lands that have drifted from their former ardor. And what America becomes largely depends upon what Americans do for the New Evangelization. This is the work God has created us to do. It is work that can give greater meaning not only to the lives of those who help, but to our own as well.

I have known Tom Peterson for many years and have seen God's work in his life and in his work — Catholics Come Home®, an international media evangelization apostolate like no other — and now in this exciting book. As I have said to him more than once, echoing the words of Mordecai to Esther, "And who knows whether you have not come to the kingdom for such a time as this?" (Est 4:14). And, dear reader, that's true not just for Tom, but also for you.

Introduction

Our family is made up of every race.

We are young and old, men and women, sinners and saints.

Our family has spanned the centuries and the globe.

With God's grace, we started hospitals to care for the sick.

We establish orphanages and help the poor.

We are the largest charitable organization on the planet, bringing relief and comfort to those in need.

We educate more children than any other scholarly or religious institution.

We developed the scientific method and laws of evidence.

We founded the college system.

We defend the dignity of all human life and uphold marriage and family.

Cities were named after our revered saints, who navigated a sacred path before us.

Guided by the Holy Spirit, we compiled the Bible.

We are transformed by sacred Scripture and sacred Tradition, which have consistently guided us for two thousand years.

We are the Catholic Church,

with over one billion in our family

sharing in the sacraments and fullness of Christian faith.

For centuries we have prayed for you and our world,

every hour of every day, whenever we celebrate the Mass.

Jesus himself laid the foundation for our faith when he said to Peter, the first pope,

"You are rock, and upon this rock I will build My Church."

For over two thousand years, we have had an unbroken line of
    shepherds
guiding the Catholic Church with love and truth in a confused
    and hurting world.
And in this world, filled with chaos, hardship, and pain,
it's comforting to know that some things remain consistent, true,
    and strong —
our Catholic faith, and the eternal love that God has for all
    creation.
If you've been away from the Catholic Church, we invite you to
    take another look.
Ours is one family united in Jesus Christ, our Lord and Savior.
We are Catholic. Welcome home.*

Not long after my awakening of faith, the epiphany that led to my faith journey, I discovered that God was also calling me to help others on their journey home. Along the way, I have also discovered that God is calling you to help love others home to the Church, too — likely in a way completely different than mine. This book is, in large part, an exploration of God's calling in your life.

I believe that deep down, most people really want to be better people and do more good in the world. Many people want to grow closer to God, to trust in him, but they just don't know where to begin. Many people begin their journey back to Jesus and the Church after being invited. This is how you can become more heroic in sharing your Catholic faith — simply by inviting someone to Mass or confession. Each of us is called by God to spread his Good News and bring souls home. After all, this is our prime mission as members of the Church, and our duty as baptized Christians. When Catholics are proud of their faith, understand their faith, and have a close relationship with Christ, our Church

---

blossoms and attracts souls.

Whether we share our beautiful Catholic faith through television and other media, or we discuss our faith with relatives, neighbors, friends, or coworkers in person, the Holy Spirit often chooses to work through faithful followers, *if we are willing.* Are you willing? Will you answer God's call to lead a more heroic Catholic life, and be a true friend and disciple of Jesus in action? If so, read on and discover God's extraordinary plan for your life and the ways in which he wants to work with and through you to bring others close to him.

CHAPTER I

Our World Needs Catholic Heroes

Few souls understand what God would accomplish in them if they were to abandon themselves unreservedly to Him and if they were to allow His grace to mold them accordingly.

SAINT IGNATIUS OF LOYOLA

I used to think a person had to be uniquely talented or special in order for God to use them; but now I know that we simply need to say *yes* to God. You see, God has something extraordinary planned for each of our lives. God has an adventure awaiting *your* life.

In our fast-paced, highly technological world, this statement might sound overly hopeful, but the lives of millions of souls who have come before us attest to this simple truth: God has a wonderful plan in store for you. God also wants you to communicate and share his extraordinary plan with the rest of the world — or at least those he puts in your path.

God also wants you to be happy. He wants you to experience his unfailing compassion. He wants you to feel the warmth of mercy and to share his love with others. God wants you to know that you exist for a reason.

It all starts with saying yes to the Holy Spirit and allowing him to guide you. Living a God-affirming life is ultimately a decision that each of us needs to make. Sometimes, it can be a tough decision. Does saying yes to God mean saying no to the secular world? To a large extent it does; but let me tell you, the exchange rate is in your favor when you trade in your old life for a new life in Christ. Remember, you simply can't out-give the generosity of God.

Particularly in today's culture, the chaos, noise, and distractions of secular society lure millions of souls away from God. Each year, this happens at an increasing rate and to more people. But it doesn't have to be that way. God is calling each of us, you and me, to bear witness to his love by leading lives of heroic virtue, sharing the Good News of Jesus with a world in need of hope, a world starving for love.

The history of the Church presents us with countless examples of men and women who led lives of extraordinary heroism. Let's look at Saint Teresa of Calcutta as one such heroic example. Mother Teresa thrived spiritually even in the squalor and uncertainty of a country where thousands died from malnutrition and hardship every day. She took what some would call the throwaways of life, people whom few thought of as human, and helped them to regain their human dignity. With trustful surrender to God's divine providence, Mother Teresa left the security of the Loreto Sisters convent in India with five rupees and wearing a sari to accept a life of poverty, living among the poorest Indians. She took up her mission in the slums of Calcutta not knowing where she would make a home or how she would survive. She put total trust in God that, because he gave her the mission, he would take care of her. Interestingly, as recent books have indicated, even Mother Teresa struggled with her faith. But you know what? She knew her purpose in life and trusted the Holy Spirit to lead the way. This isn't to say she didn't have moments when she may have struggled or doubted; yet she consistently maintained a clear vision of what she had to do: love and serve God and others. Each of us is also called to love and serve. It is God's will for his children. It's God's will for me. It's God's will for you.

You Can Become a Hero of the Faith

Granted, Mother Teresa is an extreme example of sacrificial love and service in a vocational calling. You probably know more people unlike her than you do people like her. You probably know people who are indifferent to the spiritual life, who have generally forgotten God and devoted themselves entirely to the pursuit of what they believe to be success and happiness. This is why I wrote this book — to share with you and the people around you proven ways to enter into a deeper relationship with God and his Church, and to help bring your relatives and neighbors home to Jesus and home to our universal Catholic family, as well. Our world truly needs more Catholic heroes at this time in salvation history, and each of us is called by God to play a role in leading others to deeper faith. As Saint Paul teaches us in 1 Corinthians 9:16, "For if I preach the gospel, that gives me no ground for boasting. For necessity is laid upon me. Woe to me if I do not preach the gospel!"

You may be asking, *why me, why now?* As Father Lawrence Lovasik teaches in his book *The Hidden Power of Kindness*: "Your mission in life should be to reconquer for God's glory, his unhappy world, and give it back to him. Each kind action you do helps restore the balance between right and wrong. You can find happiness only by resisting the unruly inclinations of your passions, not by serving them."

The core mission of this book is to help you become a lay witness of the New Evangelization. What does this mean? Being a lay witness of the New Evangelization is about breaking out of your nine-to-five routine in order to live a more heroic Catholic life — a destiny designed not just for priests and nuns, nor intended just for deacons and monks, but also for you and me, the ordinary folks in the pews. We must be witnesses who attest to the wonders of being in a covenant relationship with the resurrected Christ, and who live as active members of his family, the Holy Catholic Church. By learning and sharing your Catholic faith, you too can experience the greatest adventure of your life as you give yourself more completely, more passionately, to the will of God and the promptings of the Holy Spirit. It all boils down to doing one thing: surrendering yourself to Divine Providence, trusting that God will provide you with everything you need.

Global Lukewarming

In order to begin on a path toward more heroic living and holiness, you must first learn your faith; after all, you cannot give what you do not have. The Most Reverend David L. Ricken, a past chairman of the U.S. Conference of Catholic Bishops Committee on Evangelization and Catechesis, said, "In order to evangelize, a person must first be evangelized. This is really at the heart of the New Evangelization." When we fill ourselves with Christ, we can then more fully and authentically share him with others.

The time for us to act is now, since the world keeps moving faster, and more and more of our loved ones are being drawn away from the Catholic Church, which was started by Jesus Christ himself. Some of our loved ones even drift away from God altogether. Atheism and agnosticism are growing at alarming rates. The Church and the world are in dire need of true Christian witnesses, authentic and dedicated heroes of the Faith, modern-day saints who will help lead more souls to heaven. You have been called to be one of these hero-saints!

Our Lord's greatest desire for you is to become a saint, that is, to be holy. In 2 Timothy 1:9, Saint Paul says, "[God] saved us and called us with a holy calling, not in virtue of our works but in virtue of his own purpose and the grace which he gave us in Christ Jesus ages ago."

Columbia magazine, a monthly publication of my brothers in the Knights of Columbus, reported that Pope Emeritus Benedict XVI said: "The greatest crisis facing our world is the absence of God. We all need God." Our mission, as the body of Christ, is to spread the Good News of Jesus to the world. When we meet our Savior face-to-face, you and I will have to give an account to God for how well we each helped in this vital effort.

The need for Christian love in our society is real, and it is serious. Our world is starving for the spiritual. At baptism, the Holy Spirit placed in each of us a type of homing device, a type of GPS — a God Positioning System, to help us find our way back to God, home to his Church. But many people have unplugged their GPS from its power source, by abandoning the Mass and the sacraments. We need to help these wandering Catholics and others to find their way home.

The Pew Research Center reports that roughly one-fifth of Americans — 21 percent — are Catholic. According to a recent Gallup Poll, only 63 percent of Catholics in the United States claim any church membership. Twenty years ago, that number was 76 percent. These changes point to a historic shift in the Church away from Catholicism and, in some cases, away from the practice of faith altogether.

Older Catholics (those age sixty and older) show the highest rates of weekly Mass attendance, at 49 percent. That number has dropped from 59 percent over the past decade. Nearly 80 percent of Catholics who have left the Church stopped practicing their faith by age twenty-three. Today, younger adults are more likely than previous generations to claim no religious affiliation at all. In 2016, 39 percent of adults ages 18–29 said they were not affiliated with any religion. Of the 19 percent in this age group who do call themselves Catholic, "the majority of these say they seldom or never attend" Sunday Mass. In fact, only 12 percent of those Catholics ages 21–29 said they attend church weekly.

"All of this comes amid a broader trend of more Americans opting out of formal religion or being raised without it altogether," the survey said. According to Georgetown, the statistics for Europe are even worse, with churches virtually empty in many countries.

This pandemic hits home for every faithful practicing Catholic, since we all have very close family members and friends who have drifted away from the sacraments, the Catholic Church, and even from God himself. We miss these loved ones, we pray for them, and we are deeply concerned for their salvation, as we should be.

A Pew Research Center study dated September 14, 2016,

shows that since 1991 there has been a 92 percent increase in the number of unchurched Americans, often nicknamed the "nones," since they don't practice any faith and identify as having none. Indifference is escalating, and more people justify being lukewarm in faith because, by comparison, so many others are doing much worse things. Another epidemic is moral relativism, whose adherents point out that people disagree on what is moral, and therefore there is no objective right or wrong; and since no one is right or wrong, they advocate that we should tolerate others' behavior even if we don't agree with it. Another growing philosophy is secular humanism, whose proponents believe that human beings are capable of being ethical and moral without religion or God. Secularism is growing across the world, where souls are falling for the distractions and materialism of this world and giving them priority over God and his teachings. Last but not least, we see agnosticism and atheism growing exponentially.

In his book *Crazy Love*, Francis Chan talks about "lukewarm" people:

> Lukewarm people say they love Jesus, and He is indeed a part of their lives. But only a part. They give Him a section of their time, their money, and their thoughts, but He isn't allowed to control their lives. Lukewarm people will serve God and others, but there are limits as to how far they will go or how much time, money, and energy they are willing to give. Lukewarm people think about life on earth much more often than eternity in heaven. Daily life is mostly focused on today's to do list, this week's schedule, and next month's vacation. Rarely, if ever, do they intently consider the life to come.

Conversely, Chan teaches Christians that "by surrendering yourself totally to God's purpose, He will bring you the most pleasure in this life and the next."

Jesus warns in Scripture that he has no place for lukewarm

people in his service (see Rv 3:16). In our world today, many people are outraged about the environmental issue of global warming. Yet far too few people are concerned about the bigger global crisis, which my daughter Katie Peterson Warner calls the global *lukewarming* of millions of souls.

Before we can be fruitful in leading people home to Jesus and his Church, we need to grow closer to God ourselves. This is where my spiritual journey and personal story come into play. For most of my life, I was a nominal Catholic. Sure, I went to Sunday Mass, prayed, and fasted and abstained on those few days during Lent prescribed by the Church. But for me, these were routines, for the most part. What was truly important to me were my family, my career, my friends, my goals. Don't get me wrong: Family, work, friends, and goals are all important, and we displease God if we neglect them. Yet Jesus instructs us that the greatest commandment is this: "You shall love the Lord your God with all your heart, and with all your soul, and with all your mind, and with all your strength" (Mk 12:30). But that is not how I loved God. He existed on the periphery of my life; I barely thought of him unless I needed something. Part of this book tells the story of how God brought me back into full communion with the Church and transformed my life. My hope is that these insights may help you discover God's plan for your life and, God willing, open an exciting new door for you, one that brings you and those around you deeper into the faith, one moment — one soul — at a time.

CHAPTER 2

A New Springtime of Hope

The greatest challenge of the day is: how to bring about a revolution
of the heart, a revolution which has to start with each one of us.

DOROTHY DAY

When God continually embraces us, and we finally choose to embrace him back, we become filled with a passion to share the Good News of Jesus with the world. After all, that is the core mission of the body of Christ. It's why the Church exists. Through our Christian baptism, you and I are commissioned to evangelize, to proclaim Jesus to the world, and to help others discover the fullness of faith; and for Catholics, that means everything that the Catholic Church has to offer.

If the thought of sharing your faith with others makes you anxious, bear with me. You do not have to quit your job or sell your home, give up your family, enter a seminary, or spend the remainder of your mortal life tucked away in a convent. While that may be the courageous path prepared for some, it's typically not the route God has designed for most regular people like you and me, who need to live in the world but who are reminded so beautifully in the Gospels that we are not to be of the world.

The path to becoming an apostle of Christ today begins with igniting a spark of passion for your faith, then adding a bit of heroism to your life. It's about climbing out of the hole of lukewarm mediocrity to live a more vibrant, committed, and passionate faith. It's about finding true purpose and meaning for your life. Remember what Pope Emeritus Benedict XVI wrote in 2010 in his post-synodal apostolic exhortation *Verbum Domini*: "We cannot keep to ourselves the words of eternal life given to us in our encounter with Jesus Christ: they are meant for everyone, for every man and woman. ... It is our responsibility to pass on what, by God's grace, we ourselves have received."

The surest route to being a more heroic Catholic today is by living God's will, trusting the Holy Spirit to guide you, using your God-given talents and interests to their fullest potential, and serving those who are struggling with faith. Ultimately, these acts of heroism lead to sainthood. Again, don't be put off by a word that may have intimidating connotations. In fact, all baptized Christians are called to be saints. Granted, few of us will ever be formally canonized by the Church; but remember that every soul in heaven is a saint. How is that so? By the simple fact that when we go to heaven, we are joined to God forever. And that is our goal — eternal salvation with all the blessed in the kingdom of heaven. Becoming a saint starts with being rooted firmly in the truths of the Faith, attending Mass, frequently receiving Jesus in the Eucharist, obeying the Ten Commandments and the teachings of the Church, studying Sacred Scripture, and availing ourselves of the Sacrament of Reconciliation when we sin and fall short.

Today there are so many people who are lost and broken. Helping these souls find their way back home is not only a duty; it is an act of mercy. It means doing what you can do to bring a soul back into a state of grace. This will not require preaching on street corners or confronting notorious sinners (again, unless God is calling you to this type of work). Instead, I'm hoping this book will help demonstrate how the right word or the right action at the right time can be instrumental in helping your relatives, friends, neighbors, coworkers, and even strangers find their way home. This book also suggests ways to circumvent roadblocks and overcome challenges that lie ahead of you in your apostolic mission to get to heaven and help bring as many people with you as possible. And finally, in reading through this book, you will pick up some valuable tools to help you grow in happiness and fortitude, to help you cross the finish line with your eyes firmly fixed on heaven every step of the way.

If this stills sounds a bit overly ambitious to you, I understand how you feel. I felt that way, too, at first. But over time, I've come to believe for myself that with God all things are indeed possible!

Detouring off the Bridge

Imagine that you are viewing a massive and beautiful bridge spanning a cavernous river gorge. On one side of the bridge is a busy city filled with millions of inhabitants, tall buildings, and various noisy commercial and passenger vehicles. On the opposite side of the bridge is a lush, peaceful tropical paradise filled with fruit trees, flowers, waterfalls, streams, and quaint cottages, but relatively few people.

At some point you realize that while numerous cars are heading toward the bridge from the city, relatively few cars are actually completing their trip over to the other side. Most of the cars are actually getting off at the very last exit before the bridge. In fact, for every twenty-four cars that approach the bridge between the city and the tropical paradise, only eight make their way across.

Why not just take the bridge to paradise? Well this, believe it or not, happens every day. What do I mean? Let me explain.

The Catholic Church serves as our wonderful bridge, a solid support structure, designed by Jesus himself, to carry us and our families away from the tumult of the world, guiding our journey home to heaven. Yet sadly, only a small percentage of travelers are actually staying on this bridge and crossing safely to the other side. Also, few observers are volunteering to help wave the caution flags, in an effort to help direct families to their ultimate destination.

It seems as if nearly all of us have friends, close relatives, neighbors, and coworkers who have veered off the Catholic bridge to try other routes. In fact, some have abandoned their faith journey altogether and are heading back to the apparent glitter of the big city. Still others just run out of gas, stalling before crossing over the spiritual bridge and ending their progress at some point along the way.

Today, many families in our world are driving along aimlessly. So many people are searching for God, looking for a retreat from the chaos, but they just don't know how to escape the urban din. Few souls truly understand that nothing other than God will satisfy their search for happiness.

But this is exactly why we must help, now! In fact, Jesus is calling all of his followers to assist him by inviting the multitudes to a better way that will eventually lead more people safely home. You and I are being called to help in this critical rescue mission for souls. And when we serve Jesus in helping these weary travelers with some needed direction, we will discover true purpose and experience real happiness in our own lives, too.

Adventures With God

At this point, I'd like to share with you a little bit about my journey, which has had its own unique path. To be honest, there was noth-

Tom, age 2, Oak Lawn, Illinois

ing all that extraordinary about my beginnings. My 1960s Midwestern Catholic middle-class upbringing was normal. In fact, it was just plain ordinary, with a stay-at-home mom, and a dad who had a stable career working for the US Postal Service as a mail carrier and then a window clerk.

It was not until I was in high school that the talents and interests that would shape my vocation started to become evident. In retrospect, I can see that God blessed me with academic abilities, public speaking skills, a logical business mind, creativity, and ambition.

These gifts would prove fruitful in college; in my first marketing and advertising jobs out of college; and, eventually, our various Christian apostolates.

Early in my advertising career, I met and married my wife, Tricia. In the years that followed, our family was blessed with three incredible and beautiful daughters. At this point in my life, I was just a lukewarm Catholic. My faith was not a high priority, particularly as my career began to advance. The pursuit of wealth, honor, power, and achievement took all of my waking hours, and I gave these things precedence over God. I had a sizable income, a big house, nice cars. Although these comforts were fun for a time, the novelty always faded, and I began to covet the next new toy that would bring me some excitement for another month or two.

Looking back, I realize that I nearly sold my soul by chasing after idols, forfeiting my peace and investing every waking moment to acquire and maintain all the trappings the world tells us are important. My days became exhausting; slowly, I was being enslaved by the desire for a bigger home, a nicer car, and even more personal success. My spiritual pilot light, ignited at baptism and fueled by the sacraments and a solid Catholic education, had nearly been extinguished. The sad fact was that I had no idea what was going on. It was all a slow fade into a strange, almost surreal fuzziness.

A few of my friends from church saw that my priorities were grossly out of order, so they invited me on a men's retreat. I had been uplifted by retreats as a teenager, but because of distractions in recent years, I hadn't made attending a retreat a priority. I was kind of ambivalent about my friends' proposition. My mind was racing with responsibilities at the time; but finally, I decided that at least getting away would be an opportunity to decompress a bit. Maybe I could get some rest. But something amazing happened on this retreat.

Before we continue, let's look at this word "retreat" for a moment. Certainly, it means going away to pray and commune with God; but as a military term, it also means "to flee." Without knowing it at the time, I needed to flee from the superficiality and chaos of my life. In a moment of pure grace, I reconnected with God. Simply put, I finally shut up and let God talk to me in the quiet of my heart, and what he told me changed my life forever.

Inspired by the Holy Spirit, my family began downsizing and simplifying our lives. When I started making room for Jesus in my heart and investing my time in other people, my true calling became evident: to use the talents with which God had blessed me for the good of the Church and the New Evangelization.

Within a few months after my reversion experience on that retreat, by the grace of God, two new media apostolates were born:

Baby Jerry, the first infant saved from abortion thanks to a virtuemedia.org pregnancy help-line commercial

VirtueMedia™, dedicated to promoting the pro-life cause; and Catholics Come Home, dedicated to advancing the New Evangelization, called for first by Pope Saint John Paul II and more recently by Pope Emeritus Benedict XVI.

To some, the glamor and fast-paced world of television production may sound exciting and impressive; but, honestly, both apostolates had humble beginnings. VirtueMedia began in our spare bedroom as a part-time effort financed for the first few years by my day job. We started by creating two pro-life ads: one to help pregnant women who were abortion-vulnerable, and the second to offer hope and healing to women who have had an abortion. I knew relatively little about unplanned pregnancies and even less about post-abortion healing. But it seemed God was calling me to use my advertising background to help promote the sanctity of life to society, and to encourage women facing unplanned pregnancies to choose motherhood or adoption for their unborn babies.

So I learned what I could, and I learned fast.

VirtueMedia aired its first commercials on Phoenix-area television stations. Our commercials offer a toll-free number (866-88-Woman) and a link to our informational website (PregnancyLine.org), both of which connect pregnant women with local pregnancy centers in their area. We had no idea what the response would be — or even whether we would get a response. About eight months after the first ad ran, I held a newborn baby, Baby Jerry, in my arms. These commercials provided the information and resources necessary to convince Baby Jerry's mother not to have an abortion. Next came Baby Ashlynn, and then many others, thanks be to God.

Back in the 1980s, John Paul II published *Christifideles Laici*, a post-synodal apostolic exhortation in which he urged the lay faithful to participate fully in their vocation to bring the message of Jesus Christ to the world, especially through modern media. Catholics Come Home was our answer to the Holy Father's call. We did not begin with a formal marketing plan, but we were filled with enthusiasm about bringing our Catholic faith to the widest possible audience. Our ads spotlight the history, beauty, spirituality, and accomplishments of our Catholic Church. The evangelization commercials, which we call *evangomercials*™, encourage viewers to seek a personal relationship with Jesus; remind them of his Divine Mercy; and teach them that Jesus came not to condemn the world, but to save it. Our goal was to draw non-Catholics and inactive Catholics home to the Church.

Led by the Holy Spirit, within the first few years after Catholics Come Home ran its first messages, more than 500,000 souls returned to the Catholic Faith, based on reports from partner dioceses. The ads aired from Seattle to Boston, from St. Louis to New Orleans, from Corpus Christi to Sacramento, from Chicago to Phoenix. Within the first few years, nearly thirty-three archdioceses and dioceses had run these "come home" invitations. In the wake of the ads, many dioceses reported notable increases in Mass attendance, averaging about 10 percent in most dioceses, rising as high as nearly 18 percent in others. When parishes asked returnees,

"Why did you come home?" the vast majority answered, "Because you invited me." Imagine how our Church would change for the better, if more readers like you would simply "invite somebody home to Mass?"

The evidence of God's mercy is overwhelming. Without God, we can do nothing; but with God, all good things are possible! Regular people like us just need to show up with our God-given talents — our "loaves and fishes" — and join our Lord's team in this vital mission to rescue souls.

You are uniquely blessed with your own set of talents, gifts, charisms, ideas, and inspirations from the Holy Spirit. You are called to serve God in your unique mission field — your workplace or school, your neighborhood, and among your family and friends. Now is the time to discover how God is calling you to participate in your own personal adventure of the New Evangelization to help Catholics come home and help all souls in the world to know the eternal love and saving power of our Lord, Jesus Christ.

God desires to fulfill the deepest longings of your heart and make your dreams come true. He is always willing and able to help you, no matter what your strengths or shortcomings, how old or young you are, whatever your income or career, regardless of where you live. Our Father truly has a wonderful, action-packed plan and purpose for your life. He will meet you where you are, at the moment you sincerely open your heart to invite him in. Saint Teresa of Ávila tells us, "Since He does not force our will, He takes what we give Him; but He doesn't give Himself completely until we give ourselves completely."

Thoughts for Reflection

What are the gifts God has given you? How can you best use your unique gifts to help Jesus save souls? Are there people in your life who might be waiting for an invitation to come home to Mass? Who are those people, and how can you extend that invitation in love?

CHAPTER 3

Downsize and Simplify

The more complete your detachment from the things of this world,
the happier you will be.

FATHER LAWRENCE LOVASIK

G od wants you to be happy — truly happy. He is your loving
Father who created you for greatness. God wants to reveal his
love to you, and in turn he wants you to share his love with others.
But there are so many obstacles that keep you (and me) from being
truly happy. All of us are carrying heavy burdens — perhaps emotional scars from childhood, or job loss, or illness, or family challenges, or anxiety about how to meet financial obligations. And
we may be a bit disappointed with ourselves that we aren't as kind,
loving, and productive as we would like to be. Is it any surprise that
we ask, "Is this all there is to life?"

These days, societal pressure to be more and more competitive
starts at a younger age. Young people can feel overwhelmed by the
pressure to excel in sports, academics, and social settings. They
yearn to fit in. Yet, there are an ever-increasing number of distractions that lure young souls away from their Christian faith — the
one area of their lives in which they can find true happiness, real
purpose, and good lifelong friends. And it only gets worse once
they join the workforce.

Once again, I am speaking now from personal experience.

35

Upon beginning my corporate career, I felt invincible. I was goal-oriented; but also, unfortunately, becoming more self-centered. And my arrogance increased when, fresh out of my business marketing education from Arizona State University, I was offered a highly lucrative job in marketing, in which I could earn more than graduates with chemical engineering degrees! Sometime around my twenty-second birthday, the debate was whether I should buy a red Ferrari or a condo. Thankfully, reason won out, and I chose the more practical condo. (Truth be told, I just didn't know how to drive the manual transmission stick shift on the luxury Ferrari!)

Two years later, I met and married Tricia, a beautiful and kindhearted physical therapist. Tricia is the greatest blessing of my life, as are our three spirited daughters: Katie, Kimberly, and Kristina. During the early years of our marriage, my income exploded beyond the six-figure threshold, and I was in the top 1 percent of wage earners that year. So, we did what any financially well-off young family would do — we began spending it. Tricia helped me design and build a custom lakefront home in a gated community outside Phoenix, Arizona. I collected classic convertible sports cars and the latest luxury sedans. While our family and friends believed we were living the American dream, down deep I knew something was missing. Something was wrong.

Upon reaching the age of thirty, I had a chronic aliment some sociologists call "affluenza," defined as "the bloated, sluggish, and unfulfilled feeling that results from efforts to keep up with the Joneses"; and "an epidemic of stress, overwork, waste, and indebtedness caused by pursuit of the American dream." My compulsion to amass more and more material stuff was simply a futile attempt to fill the void in my heart, a void that could only be fulfilled by Jesus. At the same time, without my realizing it, God faded even more into the background. Jesus wasn't really a full-time part of my moral compass either, and the Catholic Faith wasn't a high priority in my life. I invested very little time in prayer, and typically would just ask God to bless *my plans*, rather than ask God in prayer what his perfect will was for me.

Ironically, I never missed Mass on Sunday — not even on vacation. Oh, you would see me there, but I was there mostly out of obligation and to continue the family tradition. For me at that time, putting in an hour at Mass on Sunday was like punching a time clock at a boring job. It was a chore and a duty, but that was it. During those sixty minutes every Sunday I would usually daydream, look around to find the familiar faces of friends and neighbors, wonder what was for lunch, and plan the remainder of my day. In spite of being physically present at Mass each week, my soul was absent, and my heart and mind were in another place altogether.

As I focused more and more on worldly success and achievement, my childhood spirituality began to dim, and the number and variety of my sins increased: pride, anger, harsh judgments of others, greed, gluttony, and so many other sins. Money and success were becoming my chief idols. I was becoming addicted to the sense of power that security and control brought me.

As my sins became habitual, and my conscience became desensitized, I fell deeper and deeper into the abyss of moral relativism, to the point where sins didn't feel wrong anymore. I justified my actions by telling myself, "You're not as bad as a lot of people in the news. After all, you're not a criminal or one of those notorious murderous sinners. Besides, a loving God will let you into heaven, especially if he grades the entrance exam on a curve!"

Then, while on that retreat on a hot June day in 1997, God mercifully reversed the direction of my life. I experienced a complete 180-degree turnaround! Sitting during a retreat prayer service, I began to feel a profound change come over me. In front of me, the Eucharistic Jesus was enthroned in a golden monstrance, and I was transfixed by the light that seemed to be emanating from the altar. Then my pastor, Father Doug Lorig, and some men from my parish prayed over me. Soon the spiritual floodgates opened, and I was bathed in God's compassion. I became aware of my shortcomings and sins. It was as if a light had been turned on to illuminate everything, providing me with a sense of clarity

I'd never experienced before. My heart felt moved — really moved — as if my soul was trying to throw off dead weight from all the materialistic burdens I had accumulated over the years. It felt like the kind of blast when someone power-washes the side of a house. It felt like being washed clean, as if I were experiencing my baptism all over again. It was like a car wash for my bug- and dirt-stained soul. Maybe I was finally understanding my baptism for the very first time. That afternoon I made a full confession and gratefully received God's forgiveness and merciful healing. This realization, this epiphany, was like a light switch being turned on. Though I would never compare myself to Saint Paul, the story of his conversion on the road to Damascus really hit home for me. I had been on the road of life and thought I was seeing clearly, only to learn that I'd been walking around blind. After this experience, I began to see priorities in a completely different way.

The Holy Spirit was giving me another chance, a complete *do-over*. In fact, God gives all of us second chances, third chances, and more, thanks to his unfailing Divine Mercy! That day I felt a bit like Ebenezer Scrooge after he had seen a vision of his own death, then realized he was still alive and had a chance to change his life. God began teaching me with incredible kindness. It was as if he was teaching, "You've got one foot in My world and one foot in the secular world. Choices are often black and white, but you're living in the gray area, mixing the two. You've been trying to have it both ways, but now you need to choose sides. Do you want to be on my team? Then follow Me, Tom. *Downsize and simplify* your life and rid yourself of those things that slow you down and don't bring you closer to Me."

All of us are on this same journey, where God calls us to shed those things that slow us down from the extraordinary adventure he has custom planned for each of our lives. Are there a few areas where you can downsize and simplify a bit more? By reducing the noise and clutter of the secular world, faithful Catholics will have more time to live God's perfect will for their lives and help lead more souls home to Jesus and his Church.

Becoming a New Creation

The Holy Spirit gave me the grace that made it easy to say yes; and when I accepted this direction, my whole life changed for the better. After my retreat, when I was thirty-five, my family, friends, and coworkers all witnessed my positive transformation. I began downsizing my ego and simplifying everything in my life. No longer would I drive ninety miles an hour on the Phoenix freeways, weaving in and out of slower traffic, thinking my appointments were more important than those of other drivers. Easing off the gas pedal literally slowed down my life. No longer would I habitually drop the F-bomb or other swear words in normal conversation.

Simplifying my life meant editing out all the nonsense I didn't need — and when I did this successfully with God's grace, daily life was less burdensome. Soon I started to treat people with more kindness, more compassion, more honesty, and more tenderness, and I became more Christ-like. Don't get me wrong: I still had my moments of failure, and still do to this day — after all, we are only human — but by the grace of God, I was a new creation. The Divine Mercy of Jesus, as well as the prayers of many faithful family members and friends, had brought about my return, my reversion to the fullness of the Catholic Faith. The Holy Spirit had guided me home, and now I felt I needed to respond out of love and gratitude by helping other souls on their journey home. We show our thankfulness to God by following his commandments and doing his will. Helping others draw closer to Christ is God's will for every Christian; and eventually, we will all have to give an account to God for how well we did this.

That retreat experience saved my soul, and maybe even my life. Shortly after the retreat, I met with Father Doug for spiritual direction. During our time together, he taught me about an important concept he called "the double-edged sword." God has blessed each of us with unique gifts and talents, Father Doug said, and often these gifts and talents are the exact weapons the devil uses to tempt us into sin. For example, someone with the gift of physical beauty may be tempted to commit the sins of vanity, lust, and pride. A person with the gift of eloquence may be tempted to use that gift to wound others by twisting words around or playing to other people's egos so as to manipulate them. If you've ever read Dante's classic poem *Inferno*, you know that hell is populated by many people who used words to deceive others.

For now, let's refocus on the gifts God has given to you and how you, too, can grow stronger in faith. As discussed earlier, I want this book to help you on your faith journey, so let's take a few moments to do a little spiritual survey right now. First off, let's start by saying a little prayer together.

Jesus, help me to trust in You and live Your perfect will.

Not so tough. Just say those words and hold them inside for a few moments. When you're ready, ask yourself two questions:

1. In what areas do I need improvement?
2. In what areas has God blessed me with gifts?

Now, think about how you can downsize and simplify your life, and improve upon your weaknesses. For instance, maybe you're impatient. What can you do to downsize that impatience? What can you do to simplify the way you respond to complex situations? Essentially, ask yourself, "What can I live without in my life?" Maybe you drop four-letter words, or you scream or talk loudly. Maybe you worry too much when, deep down, you know that God will provide, and you just can't seem to let go of the anxiety or the need to be in control of everything. Most of us are carrying around a bunch of extra baggage in our life. It's almost as if we're Christmas trees that are adorned with too many gaudy ornaments, added weight and clutter we just don't need and can't support. Here we are, alive and doing our work, when something happens. Rather than going to Jesus, the Prince of Peace, for help, we respond to life's challenges in a warped, inferior way that makes our lives even more burdensome. So we begin to adorn ourselves with a few heavy balls of tension, and then a few rows of electrified words, and then we string along a few boxes of tinseled yelling. What do we have? Well, a pretty sad, ugly, and chaotic-looking Christmas tree, and a life out of control.

Meditate on these words of Pope Saint John Paul II: "It is necessary to awaken again in believers a full relationship with Christ. ... Only from a personal relationship with Jesus can an effective evangelization develop."

Do not make the mistake of thinking that it is all up to you to bring about changes in yourself and others. Far from it! We all need help. And that help is found only in the Blessed Trinity and in the teachings of the Church. There are so many opportunities for us to learn from those who have come before us. Who better to teach us than Jesus and his family of saints, our cousins in the Catholic Faith, who battled shortcomings and sins and followed a successful path to holiness. So ask for their help, too. Pray that prayer:

Jesus, help me to trust in You and live Your perfect will.

Remember: Ultimately, it is our Heavenly Father, Jesus, and the Holy Spirit who convert hearts, not you and me. So pray to the Holy Spirit for guidance. Ask for his direction on how you can best use your gifts and talents to help others to come home, and for wisdom to downsize and simplify all areas of your life that keep you from growing in faith. Always remember that it is God and his holy angels who do the heavy lifting. And that's a good thing. Have you ever seen the wings on Saint Michael the Archangel? He's got to have some strong back muscles to keep those massive wings in the air!

For God is at work in you, both to will and to work
for his good pleasure.
PHILIPPIANS 2:13

Thoughts for Reflection

Now is a good time to ask yourself: What will help me grow closer to Christ? What seems to impede my spiritual progress? Where do I spend much of my time? Is that investment of time helping me to live a holier life? Eliminate the time you waste on trivial or even hurtful distractions, and you may find the time for daily Mass, praying a daily Rosary, and spiritual reading. Instead of wasting time "decompressing" by watching hours of television and surfing the Web when you get home after a hard day at work, or after you put the kids to sleep, why not spend that time reading the Bible for a few minutes, or do as Jesus told us to do — go to your room and, in the quiet and solitude, pray to your Father. Think about it. If you added just fifteen minutes of prayer to your day every day, at the end of the year you would have spent nearly four days in prayer. Now four days may not sound like a lot, but ask yourself how much time you are really giving to God every year. For many people in the world, it's closer to four minutes than four days. Downsize and simplify the distractions and chaos in your life, and replace that time with more prayer.

By doing this, we will grow closer to Christ, and be better able to reflect his light onto others who may have drifted from their faith. We can't share what we don't have; so the more we reflect the image of Christ, and the more others see Jesus in us, the more souls will be drawn toward this light of truth, hope, and love that only comes from God.

CHAPTER 4

We Just Can't Look Back

Blessed is the man who endures trial, for when he has stood
the test he will receive the crown of life which God has promised to
those who love him.

JAMES 1:12

During my undergraduate years, while I was studying business at Arizona State University, I enrolled in a psychology course called "The Rat Lab." Among other things, we learned about behavior modification by training a large black sewer rat to press a lever, which turned on a light in its cage. The rat was rewarded with a drop of water or bit of food. During the second half of the course, all the students in the class were instructed to apply this behavior modification technique in their lives in order to help correct a flaw in their character. For my experiment, I decided to train myself not to hit the snooze button, but to get out of bed as soon as my alarm sounded. Getting up immediately each morning was difficult; in the cold, dark hours of the early morning, it was tempting to roll over and sleep a little longer.

Looking back on that psychology class, I see how well those lessons prepared me for my spiritual walk in life. Following the retreat that changed my life, many times I resolved to spend more time reading the Bible, to go to Mass during the week and always on Sunday, to pray the Rosary daily, and to allocate time for morning prayer. I would begin with the best intentions; but invariably, within days of starting I would find some reason to try to justify why I couldn't continue. I think we've all been in that situation. Somehow, we fall short, and, in spite of our desire to grow closer to Christ, we allow distractions and a lack of discipline and willpower to thwart our plans. Hall of Fame football coach Bear Bryant said it well: "It's not the will to win that matters, everyone has that. It's the will to prepare to win that matters."

So, how can we develop a more disciplined focus on God, a more dedicated prayer life, and a *will to prepare to win?* I recommend two things.

First of all, we have to die to ourselves. You're probably saying, "Well, Tom, that's it, huh? That's all I have to do is die?!" Well, not literally, so let me explain.

How often are you driven by your own wants and desires? Be honest. Come on, now. The correct answer is, nearly all the time. We have basic human needs. We need food, shelter, sleep, and, to be perfectly frank, we want to feel accepted by others, too. Whether or not acceptance is a good thing or a bad thing, we need it nonetheless. We need to know that we belong and that we matter.

But what I mean when I say you have to die to yourself is that you have to shift your priorities and your focus away from yourself and onto God and others. It means setting aside your own wishes and wants in order to serve our Lord and others as best you can. This is also called "being docile to the Holy Spirit." Is it difficult? Sure, at first, but many people out there do it instinctually; namely, good parents. Anyone who has children knows that a part of you dies when your child is born. That old life in which you did whatever you wanted whenever you wanted to is essentially over. You shift focus. You serve. You provide. You love. You do what God does. Though it's tough to feel this way when your child is keeping you up at three a.m. with a stomachache, children are the greatest blessings, because they give us insight into and practice with how God, our Father, treats us.

The stories of the saints are filled with examples of selflessness.

Consider Saint Thérèse of Lisieux. In her quiet life in her convent, she had many opportunities to grow closer to God by dying to herself, growing in humility, and "becoming little" as she called it. Chore time with the other sisters provided plenty of opportunities for this. One of her most famous examples of this was when she was on laundry duty. A fellow nun was washing out handkerchiefs, and she would often carelessly splash dirty water onto Thérèse. Rather than getting angry or seeking revenge, Thérèse offered this little suffering up to God, as a means to grow in patience with the faults of others. She would often push down a bead on a string in her pocket, to signify the little offering to God. This method of dying to self in the small events of ordinary life became known as Thérèse's "Little Way" to grow in holiness. Today, we venerate Saint Thérèse of Lisieux as a Doctor of the Church, for dying to herself so well, and teaching us to do the same.

The second thing you must do is take advantage of the tremendous graces available to you in the sacraments, especially Holy Communion. One famous sage said, "Once you understand the Eucharist, you can never leave the Church. Not because the Church won't let you, but because your heart won't let you."

Sadly, according to a 2019 Pew study, 69 percent of Catholics reported that they thought the Eucharist is just a symbol, not the true Body and Blood, Soul and Divinity of Jesus Christ. Yet, Jesus himself taught his followers that we must eat his flesh and drink his blood — not symbolically, but literally. He said, "Truly, truly, I say to you, unless you eat the flesh of the Son of man and drink his blood, you have no life in you; he who eats my flesh and drinks my blood has eternal life, and I will raise him up at the last day. For my flesh is food indeed, and my blood is drink indeed" (Jn 6:53–55).

Then the Gospel of John recounts: "After this many of his disciples drew back and no longer went about with him" (6:66). You see, many disciples left because they just couldn't accept that Jesus was asking us, his disciples, to consume him in body, blood, soul, and divinity. If Jesus was giving us his Body and Blood merely as a symbol, the followers would not have found this teaching hard, nor would they have left him. Today, many people leave the Catholic Church, not understanding the True Presence of Jesus in the Sacrament of Holy Communion. Jesus did not call the disciples back, saying, "My body and blood are only meant to be understood as a symbol"; rather, he affirmed that this teaching was difficult to accept. Faith gives us the lens by which we can trust this Eucharistic teaching of Christ and his Church.

Saint Angela of Foligno is very eloquent on this topic: "If we but paused for a moment to consider attentively what takes place in this Sacrament, I am sure that the thought of Christ's love for us would transform the coldness of our hearts into a fire of love and gratitude."

Personally, I don't think it's a coincidence that I was in the presence of the Blessed Sacrament when my reversion began. Really, I didn't have much to do with it. All I did was show up, and the Holy Spirit did the rest. There will be plenty of times when we go to Communion or confession and nothing seems to happen. Sometimes, we leave Mass or confession feeling not much better off than we were before we entered the church. Yet I've learned to believe more fully in what the Nicene Creed calls the "visible and the invisible." Just because I can't always see or feel a visible change doesn't mean that an unseen transformation isn't occurring inside my soul. Think of dropping a seed into good soil. You come back the next day, and nothing appears different. The day after that, nothing new. The day after that, the same. Well, you get the picture. But a couple of weeks later, you start to see a sprig of life pushing out of the ground! Aha, new life. What Dante called *la vita nuova*!

Trusting in God is easier said than done. Well, sure it is. I'm not going to lie to you. It takes effort and practice and discipline. So do all great things in life. That's just the way it is. But it can be done. The saints prove that it is possible to honor Our Lord and love and serve him with "all your heart, and with all your soul, and with all your strength."

Right about now you're probably thinking that it was easier for the saints in centuries past, when society was not so corrupt and aggressively secular, when life wasn't so complicated, when there were fewer temptations. Any student of history can tell you that times have always been difficult, and Scripture confirms: "There is nothing new under the sun" (Eccl 1:9). It is important to remember that you are called to be holy at this time in history, precisely in the place that God has planted you, with the talents he has given you. When you live your life centered on Christ, others will be drawn to this authentic witness and may ask the reason for your hope (see 1 Pt 3:15).

Now, just a warning: At times, there will be roadblocks. The devil is constantly trying to trip us up, to distract us from God, to get us to take our eyes off heaven. He knows each of our specific and most vulnerable weaknesses and will dish up customized temptations in an effort to get each one of us to fall, to drift away from God and turn back to our former lives. He doesn't want us to become holy. And the devil certainly doesn't want us to be saved, or to help others be saved. He is a liar, a deceiver, and incapable of love. But he wants our souls more than anything else, and he'll stoop to anything to get them. I often say, the devil has custom-made fishing lures, trying to snare each one of us. His minions are constantly whispering thoughts into our ears, without us realizing it. (Author and Christian speaker Joyce Meyer wrote a great book called *Battlefield of the Mind* that can help you fight this spiritual warfare.)

Before leaving the retreat, I had committed myself to going to Mass each morning at my neighborhood parish at that time, St. Anne in Gilbert, Arizona. It was at daily Mass that I felt God was re-forming me, teaching me, healing me. As I started to learn, or rather relearn, my Catholic faith, I began to truly appreciate as if for the first time the Mass, the Eucharist, adoration of the Blessed Sacrament, the Sacrament of Reconciliation, the Rosary and Chaplet of Divine Mercy, the sacrifice of Jesus for my sins, and the example and intercession of the Blessed Mother and the saints.

The Bible became the inspiring road map for my life. It had

just what I needed to navigate the obstacles in my personal and my professional life. Whenever I needed them most, God's words from Scripture would come to mind. On many busy mornings, as I was on my way to Mass, I would debate skipping Mass that day and going straight to work. Then the following words would resonate in my mind: "Seek first his kingdom and his righteousness, and all these things shall be yours as well" (Mt 6:33). So I went to Mass. Once I trusted in Jesus, my work days went exceedingly well. All the knots were unknotted. Everything ran much more smoothly. The other two Scriptures that continued to surface in my heart were: "The harvest is plentiful, but the laborers are few" (Mt 9:37); and "Every one to whom much is given, of him will much be required" (Lk 12:48). I knew I needed to keep moving forward with God.

At this time, I was also growing to love the gentle, uncomplicated theology of Saint Thérèse of Lisieux, a.k.a., the Little Flower. Saint Thérèse, a Doctor of the Catholic Church, was a young Carmelite nun who developed a method for growing in holiness that she called "the Little Way" (mentioned earlier). She taught that even the most mundane task, if done for love of God, is pleasing to him and helps us grow in holiness. Her method could be summed up with a quote that has often been attributed to her: "At every moment, do what love requires." Saint Thérèse's simple, yet profound, Little Way has appealed to Catholics around the globe. Since her canonization in 1925, she has been one of the most beloved saints.

By studying the saints, our brothers and sisters who have gone before us, I realized how much they could enrich my life. The saints have become my spiritual guides, and I have come to realize how desperately I need their guidance as mentors who truly navigated the path before us. They can serve as true mentors on our spiritual walk.

The time immediately after my "reversion" was like a honeymoon, but that did not last. One day the headline on the front page of the *Phoenix New Times* read: "White-collar Criminals." The story referred to an investigation into the business practices of

my biggest television client. Given their unethical business practices, I felt I could not work with this client any longer. Dropping
this business would mean a major financial sacrifice for me and
my family, as the fees from this client constituted one-third of my
annual income.

What should I do? Here was the first major test of my newly
rediscovered faith, and I did not make my decision until I was pull-
ing into my client's parking lot. I decided to honor God by severing
my business relationship with this client so as not to "yoke" myself
with unbelievers.

In addition to promising to attend daily Mass, I had made
another promise to God: I vowed to be more generous in my gifts
to charity. God had been blessing me and my family with a significant income, yet each week I was putting only a couple dollars into
the collection basket. Now that I understood that all my blessings
had come from the Lord, I was eager to demonstrate my gratitude
by writing a check in five figures, to represent a 10 percent tithe, a
gift of our first fruits back to God as discussed in Scripture. Within just minutes after my television client and I went our separate
ways, doubt entered my mind, and I heard: "You can't afford to
write such a large check to charity. You've lost one-third of your
income! You have a wife and three young girls at home to take care
of. Don't you want to be a good husband and father?" Amazingly,
for the first time in my life, I discerned that this was *not* God's
whisper; it was the noise of the one Jesus called "the father of lies"
(Jn 8:44). Before any second thoughts could take hold, I drove
straight to my parish and wrote the generous check, giving God
back a portion of which he generously gave me earlier. Leaving the
parish office a little shaken, I still knew in my heart that God was
guiding me in the right direction, and that if I continued to try to
grow closer to God through attending Mass, receiving the sacraments, and praying frequently, I would remain on the right path.

However, there was more pruning to be done. Other business
clients and even some of my colleagues tried to entice me back
into my old sinful life. I could not risk the temptation and pulled

back from these business associates, too. Soon my small advertising agency was left with just one client that was generating a paltry three hundred dollars a month in income, not the tens of thousands a month I had grown accustomed to.

During the retreat, I had come to understand that the clutter of our possessions can distract us from time we should be spending with God. So Tricia and I put our second home, a vacation home in Flagstaff, Arizona, up for sale. Easy, right? Well, just wait — there is more to this story!

One night, not long after we decided to sell the house, we received a phone call from a friend. He and his family were staying at our Flagstaff mountain home. They had been out for the day, and when they returned, they found that a car had crashed through the front of our house and come to a stop right in the middle of our kitchen! Thank God, our friends were not in the house at the time. No one was hurt. In fact, there was no driver in the car. You see, a high school girl, who was responsible for the car, had been visiting friends up the street and had forgotten to put on the parking brake. Her car had rolled briskly down the hill, straight into our kitchen.

The next morning, I made the two-hour drive up into the mountains to assess the damage. The insurance adjuster was waiting for me in the driveway, along with the high school girl and her mother. Soon, about a dozen of our neighbors came over. The girl sobbed as she asked for my forgiveness. Her mother was concerned that I might have intended to file a lawsuit, but I assured her that was never a consideration for me. "It's okay," I said to the girl. "It was an accident."

"Why aren't you mad at me?" the girl asked.

"Well," I said, "a couple weeks ago I would have been very upset, and would have come unglued. But I just went on a retreat with my parish where I felt God's love and mercy like never before. I'm beginning to see things differently now. You made a mistake, and I certainly want you to know I understand, and I forgive you."

In 1 Peter 3:15 we read, "Always be prepared to make a defense to anyone who calls you to account for the hope that is in you, yet do it with gentleness and reverence." That brief statement in the driveway was my first "elevator pitch" for my faith — a concise, personal testimony of the undeniable and remarkably tangible positive place that Christianity now occupied in my life.

As you also begin to draw people back to the Church, you'll discover that the trials and triumphs you experience on your faith walk matter to other people, because they are experiencing the same setbacks, failures, successes, and joys. The best evangelizers are good at what they do, because they make an effort to relate to their audience by sharing their common life experiences.

That unfortunate event at our vacation home taught me a valuable lesson: We must learn to praise God in all things, even our trials. Had I not accepted God's will or grace to calm my heart on that retreat, then when I heard the bad news about my vacation home, those dozen people might not have heard the Good News about Jesus, and how faith changes lives.

That accident taught me to surrender to Divine Providence. It taught me patience and obedience. It taught me not to look back at my old way of living. And, it presented me with an opportunity to give testimony to a dozen neighbors about God's plan for our happiness. As Saint Paul reminds us in Romans 8:28, "We know that in everything God works for good with those who love him, who are called according to his purpose." And Psalm 112:7 reminds us, "His heart is firm, trusting in the Lord."

Following these events, God's amazing plan for me began to come into clearer focus. I understood that I was being called upon to center my life on God, to work to help Catholics to come home to the Church, and never to look over my shoulder with longing upon what might once have seemed to me to be the "glamour" of my old passions.

In his book *Love Does*, Bob Goff shares this wisdom: "I used to think I could shape the circumstances around me, but now I know Jesus uses circumstances to shape me." God shapes each of us so that we are inspired to live like him, serve him, and lead others to encounter his merciful love.

*Normally Our Lord asks us to give a Christian witness through
our ordinary lives, engaged in the same ways of earning a living,
tackling the same concerns as other folk. We have to act in such a
way that others will be able to say, when they meet us: This man
is a Christian, because he does not hate, because he is ready to understand, because he is not a fanatic, because he is willing to make
sacrifices, because he shows that he is a man of peace, because he
knows how to love.*

FRANCIS FERNANDEZ, IN CONVERSATION WITH GOD

Thoughts for Reflection

"How are you?"

In our fast-paced world, that question has become a sort of
verbal filler. We say it to colleagues, people who help us at the
checkout counter, even the grump behind the window at the DMV.
Most of the time people don't answer, or they'll give us a one-word
answer: "Fine." You know how many times I've heard someone
respond, "Fine"? If people's lives were this fine, we wouldn't be in
half the messes we are in today!

So, here's something to think about. The next time you greet
someone, put a little spirit behind that question — even allow the
Holy Spirit to articulate the words for you. Show a little enthusiasm. And when someone asks, "How are you?" answer them,
"I'm blessed. How are you?" If the person you're speaking with is a
Christian, your reply will remind them that we are all connected as
members of God's family. If they are not deep in faith, your answer
may get them thinking about God and the many blessings they
have received. This response often leads to interesting conversations and, occasionally, an opportunity to pray with someone who
is in need of hope.

As Pope Emeritus Benedict XVI said to a congregation in Genoa in 2008, "Help each other to live and to grow in the Christian faith so as to be valiant witnesses of the Lord. Be united, but not closed. Be humble, but not fearful. Be simple, but not naive. Be thoughtful, but not complicated. Enter into dialogue with others, but be yourselves."

Fast Before You Feast

*Freedom consists not in doing what we like, but in having the right
to do what we ought. ... There is no evil to be faced that Christ
does not face with us. There is no enemy that Christ has not already
conquered. There is no cross to bear that Christ has not already
borne for us, and does not now bear with us.*

POPE SAINT JOHN PAUL II

A s you progress on your journey of faith, by building a firm
foundation on Christ and helping others to return to the
Church, you will find it necessary to fend off distractions and
pull up the weeds that threaten to choke your spiritual progress.
Each of us has a unique set of sins, bad habits, "rocks and thorns"
that can be eliminated only with God's grace and our diligence
and discipline. In the Parable of the Sower in the Gospel of Mark
(4:1–20), Jesus likens humankind to a fertile field and the message
of the Gospel to seed. Some people ignored Christ and his message entirely. Others were enthusiastic for a time, but soon their
faith withered away. Some of them had faith, but it was choked
by thorns, the temptations of the world. But some seeds "fell into
good soil and brought forth grain, growing up and increasing and
yielding thirtyfold and sixtyfold and a hundredfold" (Mk 4:8). To
grow in holiness, a Christian soul needs good soil and a firm root
system, and the best way to acquire both is through the Mass, the

sacraments, and regular prayer.

It takes discipline to maintain a life of prayer; but while you are nurturing your soul, remember that you are also responsible for keeping your body healthy. When beginning this mission, I realized that I wasn't exercising, sleeping, or eating in a very disciplined manner, and that some changes were in order if I wanted to have the health and the strength necessary to fulfill the task God had given me. Keep your mind, body, and soul in harmony so that you can serve the Lord and fulfill your God-given roles.

We become what we surround ourselves with — the books we read, the friends we keep, the TV shows we stream online, and the amount of time we devote to God and the sacramental life. As you develop patterns of good spiritual behavior, you will find it easier to resist temptations and live a healthier life as well.

Just a quick aside, while we're talking about temptations: I would guess that oftentimes we are tempted, even as faithful Catholics, to ask, "What is the very least I can do to get into purgatory?" Too often I have been guilty of settling for purgatory! Seems like we just want to make the cut, get into this waiting room of heaven, with the least effort or sacrifice. God doesn't want us to settle for a life of mediocrity, but to love him with all our heart, mind, soul, and strength. Father Mark Beard, a late vocation priest from Baton Rouge, Louisiana, once said, "If we aim for purgatory and miss, what do we get? It's hell! But if we aim for heaven and fall short, at least we end up in purgatory!" See how critical it is to keep our focus on the goal, fixing our eyes on more than the consolation prize! We must constantly gaze upward, seeking heaven. If we don't, we can be caught in the whirlpool of moral relativism and secularism.

When I was in prep school, one of the math teachers presented the class with two options: Would we rather have ten thousand dollars today or a penny today that doubles in value every day for the next thirty days? So one penny doubles to two, two cents doubles to four, and so on over thirty days. Most of my classmates took the quick cash, the instant gratification, but in doing so they settled for much less than the $1.7 million payoff from that penny that kept doubling daily for thirty days.

We can bear this lesson in mind when it comes to spreading the Faith. Imagine that you become the best person of faith you can become, and you reach out to one Catholic who may be wavering in his or her faith, and you help that person. Then that person reaches out to one Catholic, and then that person reaches out to another Catholic ... well, there's no telling where this domino effect of goodwill would end, but I have a hunch that soon Sunday Mass would be a lot more crowded.

The same is true in your private life. You could spend a couple of hours watching television tonight, or you could read a great Catholic book that will help you grow in faith. You could text your friends, or you could say a Rosary for someone who needs your prayers. And imagine how your life would change for the better if you dedicated just one hour a week to Eucharistic adoration.

John Paul II spent a good part of his pontificate reminding us to go deeper into our faith and to keep our focus on Jesus. Remember the story in Matthew 14:22–33 of Peter walking on water toward Christ? One night, Peter was fishing with some of the apostles when they saw Christ walking toward them on the water. Suddenly filled with zeal, Peter asked Jesus if he could walk across the water to meet him. "Come," Jesus said. So Peter climbed out of the boat and began to walk on the water. When he became afraid, he took his focus off Christ, got distracted, and began to sink. "Lord, save me," Peter cried. Jesus grabbed his hand and pulled him up, and together they stepped into the boat. "O you of little faith," Jesus said, "why did you doubt?"

When we take our eyes off Jesus, we always sink. God reminds us to make choices that will nourish our souls, such as frequent attendance at Mass, frequent reception of the sacraments, spending more time in prayer and reading the Bible, and being more generous in serving others who are in need. Like taking daily doses of vitamins and eating a healthy diet, all these religious practices add up, feeding our souls, helping us to stay close to Christ, and enabling us to grow in holiness. In the tumult of each day, we can be tempted to avert our gaze from Christ and back to our short-term comforts, financial security, and our focus on doing our own will. As Proverbs 4:23 reminds us, "Keep your heart with all vigilance; for from it flow the springs of life." Jesus also calls us to help lead souls to him. We are better equipped to do this when our faith is healthy, and we are not impeded by sin that weighs us down and distracts us from this mission.

From time to time, we are called to sacrifice something we want. Often, this is an invitation from God to turn away from one of the petty pleasures offered by secular society and discover the "pearl of great price," the source of lasting happiness, Jesus Christ. When we make this choice, we are heading toward the greatest good. You and I are called through baptism to become heroes of the Faith. With more faithful apostles serving Christ and helping others, our society will truly blossom.

Trustful Surrender

In 2012, I was approached by a nice lady after morning Mass at my parish of St. Peter Chanel in Roswell, Georgia. She recognized me from my television series, but also had met me years earlier, when I lived in Arizona. She asked whether I had heard about what happened to Jeff Van Brunt, my first Phoenix area VirtueMedia (pro-life) employee, who served with me years ago. After hearing his story, I asked Jeff to meet me at the studio, and to sit and chat with me on camera, unscripted. Our conversation turned into an

Jeff and his wife, Jill, early in their marriage. Watch Jeff's inspirational television special on YouTube, entitled Trustful Surrender to God!

hour-long international TV special, aired on EWTN worldwide each Lent, called "Trustful Surrender to God."

Jeff Van Brunt was about thirty-one years old, the father of four children with a beautiful wife, Jill. Jeff had an amazing career in nonprofit education service for Great Hearts Academy over the past years. A few minutes into the interview, Jeff dropped the bomb, saying, "I have ALS, Lou Gehrig's disease." He explained that when properly diagnosed, people die within three to five years. Then Jeff shocked me, our film crew, and eventually our worldwide viewing audience by saying, "I thank God I have ALS."

What! Who would *thank* God for such a terminal diagnosis? Jeff went on to explain that he had not really been leading a faithful Catholic life. He had drifted into some sins common to men his age. His ALS diagnosis led him to understand his true purpose in life, his mission from God — to love and serve God and others with all his heart. Jeff went on to say, "Sin weighs us down, slows us down from doing our mission that God has appointed each of us to do."

About eight years after his diagnosis, Jeff went to his eternal reward. All of us at his funeral spoke of how we witnessed a true saint among us, who heroically carried his cross out of love of God and service to others. Jeff taught so many of us the true meaning of evangelization, through his years of vocational service, and mostly by his faithful example of carrying a very heavy cross with such faith, hope, and love over the finish line, into the next life! He evangelized thousands through his work, from the caretakers at his bedside to family members and friends, and even a worldwide television audience.

As Jeff exemplified, when you reach out to the under-churched and the unchurched, you cannot know the impact you may have on their lives, their souls, their families. Parents who rarely, if ever, take their children to Mass may, through your efforts, bring their family back into the Church. You may do something that will affect that family for generations. Do not be shy about sharing the mercy of Jesus with others. Never give up, because countless souls are depending on you. In 2006, while speaking to bishops from Ontario, Pope Benedict XVI pinpointed why evangelization is so vital: "The fundamental task of the evangelization of culture is the challenge to make God visible in the human face of Jesus," he said.

If you invite someone to return to the Church and your invitation is rebuffed, don't despair. Pray instead. The best thing you can do for those who are away from the Church is to listen to them; show them love; and, most of all, pray for them. At times prayer can seem so inconsequential, but it has very real effects. Big things happen when you pray. History and the lives of the saints verify this truth again and again. Consider the example of Saint Monica. Although she tried to raise her son Augustine as a Christian, when he went away to university he joined a pagan cult and took a mistress. Monica prayed ceaselessly for her son to come to the fullness of the Catholic Faith. It seemed hopeless, but after almost twenty years, the once promiscuous, proud, obstinate Augustine repented. He went on to become a priest, a bishop, and a theologian. In fact, the theological writings of Saint Augustine are among the most influential in the history of the Church, second only to the epistles of Saint Paul the Apostle. And while all the credit goes to God, you have to believe there was great power in Saint Monica's prayers.

We have to show everyone that Christ is still alive by living heroically the events of our daily lives. The apostolic vocation which we all received at Baptism means giving witness in word and deed to the life and teaching of Christ. People said of the early Christians, see how they love one another! The pagans were really edified by this behavior and those who conducted themselves in this way had favor with all the people, as the Acts of the Apostles tell us.

FRANCIS FERNANDEZ, IN CONVERSATION WITH GOD

Thoughts for Reflection

God calls his disciples to choose the greatest good, the long-term benefit, and to fast before we feast. Archbishop Fulton Sheen once said: "Never forget that there are only two philosophies to rule your life: the one of the cross, which starts with the fast and ends with the feast. The other of Satan, which starts with the feast and ends with the headache."

What can you fast from today, that will make it possible for you to feast later in your spiritual life? What small actions can you take every day to grow in faith? I am a firm believer that where you put your focus is where you end up in life. If you're driving a car, and you mistakenly focus on the wall in a long tunnel, and not on the road in front of you, well, you're going to slam into that wall. In the same way, we should wake every day with the intention of putting aside something that doesn't help us grow closer to Christ and our goal of heaven. When you begin to focus on the longer term benefits of growing in faith, guess what? You'll start doing just that! I think that one of our greatest failings isn't that we're bad people or that we do bad things, but that we forget very easily to keep focused on our ultimate goal of heaven, and the discipline of doing more good things. It's easy to make a commitment to change your life. It's another thing to remember to pray for God's gift of grace so you will stick to that commitment with fortitude. So keep that in mind when you wake up every morning: Discipline yourself to journey deeper into your faith; then you will also be more effective in helping others to come home to Christ.

CHAPTER 6

If You Love Me,
Feed My Sheep

*[Jesus said,] "Follow me and I will make you
become fishers of men."*

MARK 1:17

A re there second chances in life? The Bible affirms that there are many second chances, thanks to the mercy of God! Consider the case of Saint Peter. He was the most prominent of the apostles, the man to whom Christ gave the keys to the kingdom of heaven, the man Christ chose to be the first pope. Peter and his fellow apostles James and John formed Jesus' inner circle; they were Our Lord's closest friends. On the night Jesus was arrested, Peter denied that he knew Jesus — and he did so within Christ's hearing. At the foot of the cross the next day, when Jesus was dying on Mount Calvary, John and the Blessed Mother were present, along with Mary's sister, Mary the wife of Clopas, and Mary Magdalene. Peter was nowhere to be found. Nevertheless, our Lord gave Peter another chance to fulfill his vocation, to live the plan that God had prepared for him.

Immediately after this triple denial, Peter was filled with remorse and ran off into the night, weeping. His contrition was sincere, and that is why, after his resurrection, Jesus showed mercy to

Peter. (Contrast this with Judas, who betrayed Jesus as well, but who never repented.) In John 21:15–17 we read that three times Christ asked Peter, "Do you love me?" Each time Peter responded, "Yes, Lord; you know that I love you." Those three statements of love canceled out the three denials Peter had made in the high priest's courtyard. In response, Christ confirmed Peter in his office as head of the Church. "Feed my lambs," Jesus said. "Feed my sheep." And that is exactly what Saint Peter did. You and I are called to feed Jesus' sheep, too.

Like Saint Peter, we are called upon to share the mystery of the divine mercy of God with others and to tell the world that we serve a God of love; who, because of his forgiving heart, is always eager to give unlimited second chances to anyone who is repentant and seeks his forgiveness.

One morning, while I was praying before Mass, I remembered that a priest had suggested that we pray every day that we might be an instrument to lead someone closer to Christ. So that morning I asked God to use me that day to bring someone — anyone, I wasn't picky — closer to his Son, Jesus. After Mass ended, the little Vietnamese lady seated next to me leaned over and asked if I would help her son. We went to the narthex to talk, so as not to disturb a group who had stayed after Mass to pray the Rosary.

With great anguish, this lady told me that her son had been away from the Church for nearly twenty years. She asked if I would invite him to Mass. It's always surprising how quickly the Lord answers our prayers when it's something he wants done. The mother added a special request — that I not tell her son that his mama had sent me, because it would embarrass him and perhaps make him angry with her. When I asked where I could meet her son, she said, "He works in a nail store." She meant that her son worked at a women's manicure salon. She told me her son's name was Jimmy. I went home, picked up some Catholic leaflets, then drove to the nail salon. Walking through the door, I spotted my friend's son immediately. I confess, I was a little nervous, but I said, "Somebody who loves you, God himself, and I want to invite you back to the Catholic Church." What followed was silence, absolute silence, for what seemed to me to be an eternity. Finally Jimmy said, "Well, it's nice of you to invite me, but I don't need church because I find God in nature. I'm a professional fisherman, and I fish nearly every day, and I feel close to God when I'm outdoors."

Not very eloquently, I agreed that we certainly can find God in nature, since God created nature. But I went on to say that Jesus gave us a Church so that we could help each other get to heaven. With the world being so complex, and life so difficult, it's important for us to stick together as a Catholic family. Furthermore, it has always been Jesus' desire that we should receive Communion and the Sacrament of Reconciliation frequently to help us on our journey.

When we said our goodbyes, I wasn't sure whether I had helped or not.

From time to time I dropped in to talk with Jimmy, and we developed a bit of a friendship. Twice I invited him to Mass, but he never showed up. Nonetheless, I tried to be optimistic. I remembered something the great Dominican preacher Saint Vincent Ferrer once said: "If you truly want to help the soul of your neighbor, you should approach God first with all your heart. Ask him simply to fill you with charity, the greatest of all virtues; with it you can accomplish what you desire." So I prayed for Jimmy with all my heart, and then I waited to see what God would do.

Finally, one Sunday morning, Jimmy called to say that he would join me at Mass that day. Given his track record, I was not optimistic, but this time he did show up. "Everything's changed," he told me. "I went fishing like I always do on Sunday morning, but this time I fished a crucifix out of the water. Do you think it was a sign?" I was both dumbfounded and elated. "God didn't just give you a cross," I said. "He gave you a Roman Catholic crucifix to show you which Church to come home to."

Then he asked, "Where is the box?" It took me a minute to realize Jimmy wanted to go to confession. I led him to the sacristy where the priest was vesting for Mass and introduced Jimmy. The priest led him to a side chapel, where he heard his confession before going to the altar to say Mass. That morning the prayers of a Vietnamese mother were answered — her son returned to the Church and the sacraments after being away for twenty years.

We stayed in touch. When Jimmy got married, Tricia and I were invited to the wedding Mass. When he got back from his honeymoon, he stopped by our house to show us the wedding photos. While Tricia and our girls were looking at the pictures, Jimmy pulled me aside into the kitchen to say, "Tom, I have something to share with you that you don't know. My mom and I are so grateful that you invited me back to church."

I replied, "You're welcome; it's no big deal."

Jimmy corrected me, saying, "Oh yes, it is a big deal, and you don't know the whole story. I was in the Asian mafia in Los Angeles and got arrested for major felony crimes against society. I went to a federal penitentiary and served my sentence for the last fifteen years." Upon hearing that, I turned ashen white and felt like all the blood had rushed out of my body. I thought to myself, "Thank goodness I didn't know about this ahead of time! I probably would have chickened out!"

Then Jimmy said, "I want to tell you, I'm so grateful, because in prison I almost committed suicide, and there were a lot of other issues. But I want you to know that in prison the inmates had time to talk about Jesus and share their faith. But now that I'm out, everybody's too busy; nobody takes the time to talk about God with other people. Thank you for taking the time to invite me back. That changed my life."

Jimmy's comments hit my heart, and I realized later that there are millions of Jimmys in the world, countless struggling souls who never grew up with much faith, or who left the Church for whatever reason. You and I need to pray for them and help these Catholics come home. We cannot be afraid to do so, as our fear of failure or fear of offending others impedes Christ's mission for the salvation of souls. The Good Shepherd reminds us that the upside of one soul responding positively and coming home to Jesus and his Church far outweighs the downside of a few people who may reject our faith-sharing overture. So what happened here? I prayed to help bring someone closer to Christ, and I was willing to serve. What happened? Jimmy's life was changed forever; and, thankfully, I got to witness this great adventure from God! This is all God's work; it had little to do with me. Through this experience I learned how powerful our willingness to serve is to God. Think of the millions of struggling souls, souls who might respond to a kind word about how much God loves them. Let's go to God for the grace to be a positive influence in the lives of these souls. Ask God for the strength, the fortitude, and the heroism to do the right thing. Seek by being present to the people around you. Knock on the proverbial doors of other people's hearts, by helping them to come closer to Christ.

Saint Paul in 2 Timothy 2:24–25 tells us: "And the Lord's servant must not be quarrelsome but kindly to everyone, an apt teacher, forbearing, correcting his opponents with gentleness. God may perhaps grant that they will repent and come to know the truth." If you are constantly getting into arguments about someone's religious practice (or lack thereof), you are obstructing your efforts to help them come home. Of course you are convinced of the truth, goodness, and beauty of the Faith, but express your conviction gently. You are called to love people into heaven, not argue them into submission. I think it's worth pointing out that sometimes we'll need to take a page from Jimmy's mother's book. She asked someone else to help when she knew her son wouldn't listen to her. Sometimes we need to do this, too, if we want to reach our loved ones!

Father Lawrence Lovasik teaches in his book, *The Hidden Power of Kindness*, "Each kind action you do helps restore the balance between right and wrong." This is exactly why we need to regularly reach out to others and invite them home to the Church.

Thoughts for Reflection

Don't try to impress others with your eloquence or win an argument with a laundry list of facts. You may win the argument, but you may also lose a friend. People want to be heard, they want to be loved, and they will be more open if they see Christ in you. So ask God for the gifts of kindness, compassion, and gentleness. Seek a way to bring these gifts to another's door, and then knock and offer these gifts in any way you can.

CHAPTER 7

Unveil the Mystery

The fundamental objective of the formation of the lay faithful is an ever-clearer discovery of one's vocation and the ever-greater willingness to live it so as to fulfill one's mission. ... The lay faithful, in fact, "are called by God so that they, led by the spirit of the Gospel, might contribute to the sanctification of the world, as from within like leaven, by fulfilling their own particular duties. Thus, especially in this way of life, resplendent in faith, hope and charity they manifest Christ to others."

POPE SAINT JOHN PAUL II

Years ago, during a motivational sales training class, the speaker drew a large iceberg on the board. Near the top he sketched in a wavy line indicating the surface of the ocean. Then he pointed to the large mass beneath the waves and asked the class, "What is this?" Someone answered, "The bottom of the iceberg." The speaker said, "Yes, but it's more accurate to say that this is the unseen potential of the iceberg. What we see is only 10 percent of the iceberg, but 90 percent of its mass is a bit of a mystery, isn't it?"

We are a lot like that iceberg: Much of who we are lies below the surface. You and I are utilizing only a fraction of the potential God has implanted in us. Imagine how our lives would change, how the world would benefit, if we began to exercise the other 90 percent of our blessings, gifts, charisms, and talents that lie below the surface of our personality.

People who are away from the Church suffer from an "iceberg mentality" with regard to the Church — they see only a fraction of what the Church has to offer; they have no idea how much more beauty and wonder lie below the surface, waiting to be explored.

Not long after my life-changing retreat, Tracey, a colleague whom I had known years before, met me for breakfast. As we were catching up on the recent events in each of our lives, I told her about my reversion experience. After I summarized some highlights from the retreat, Tracey mentioned that although she was raised Lutheran, some of her other family members had been Catholic, and occasionally she had thought about becoming a Catholic, too. This led us into a deeper conversation about the Church and the Faith.

A few months later, Tracey enrolled in the Rite of Christian Initiation of Adults (RCIA) at a Catholic parish. Even before she was received into the Church, she had become an enthusiastic novice Catholic evangelist. One evening she called to ask if I would be willing to speak with a friend of hers, Michael, who had drifted away from the Church. This was only a few months after my reversion, so the idea of speaking about the Faith with a complete stranger made me a bit uncomfortable. Nonetheless, I agreed to speak with Michael. I thought I would just speak from my heart and trust that God would give me the right words to say.

The next day, Michael called. The prospect of talking about such a delicate topic as faith with a stranger had made me ill at ease; but with God's help, the conversation flowed naturally. After a forty-five-minute conversation, he said, "I'm coming back. I've needed to do this for years, and I'm convinced the good Lord is inviting me back." That was an exciting moment. Michael had made a life-changing decision, and I was grateful and humbled that the Holy Spirit had permitted me to be an instrument in his return to the Church.

Tracey called to thank me for talking to Michael. She mentioned how excited he was about coming back to the Church after having left when his children were still very young. But when Tracey called again two days later, her voice sounded very somber. She began by saying, "Thanks again for helping Michael, but I've got some bad news to tell you. He *died* this morning!"

In complete shock and disbelief, I said, "The guy I just talked to on the phone two days ago?"

"Yeah, he just died," Tracey repeated. It was hard to comprehend that this nice guy had died so suddenly. Tracey continued, "But here's why I'm calling you. Not only to tell you this news — and I am grateful that you helped Michael — but we need to help his family now. They haven't been going to Mass for years either, but they want Michael to have a Catholic funeral. It's kind of complicated. The priest said he can do the wake at the funeral home, but he can't preside at the interment, due to another commitment that afternoon. He told me a layman would be allowed to say the committal prayers at the graveside, so will you do this service for the family?" I thought Tracey was kidding. Nevertheless, I agreed to help in any way possible.

Out of obedience to Church teachings, I wanted to double-check with my pastor regarding a layperson leading a graveside service. So the next morning after Mass, I went into the sacristy and asked Father Doug if this was permissible. When he said it was, I started to feel clammy all over. "Well, what do I do and what prayer book do I use?" I asked. "Don't I need to sprinkle holy water to bless the coffin and grave?" After some simple coaching from Father Doug, I called Tracey to confirm that I would lead the burial prayers. Again, this was really pushing me beyond my comfort zone, but it seemed that Michael's family didn't have any other, better options.

"Wait, there's another strange wrinkle to the story," Tracey said. "Michael's son, Keith, had just been put in jail yesterday night. He was accused of *murder*. His sister, Heather, asked if you and I could go to the jail with her to tell Keith that his dad died." I told my wife what had happened, then climbed into my car headed for the county jail in downtown Phoenix. The adrenaline was pumping in my veins, but I also felt simultaneously so nauseous and nervous.

At the jail, Tracey explained the circumstances of Michael's sudden death to the clerk and introduced me as the family's spiritual adviser. Before entering the area where the inmates were held, I was required to remove my watch and my wedding ring and put them, along with my wallet, in a basket; I could claim my belongings when I was ready to leave the building. At that moment I felt bare and somewhat helpless.

As we walked down the narrow, gray halls, my stomach churned. More than at any other time in my life, I felt completely out of my element. We were led into a large room with several tables and picnic-style benches. Heavy iron bars covered all the windows. The guard instructed us to sit and wait at one of the tables. After the longest ten minutes of my life, we heard the clanking of bars and steel doors, and then a guard brought Keith into the room and led him to our table. His sister sat quietly on one end of the bench, Tracey in the middle, with me seated on the other end. His sister sobbed, and with a shaky voice she told her brother that their dad had passed away after a massive heart attack. As she was telling him the horrific news, Keith looked at me and said, "Who the hell are you?"

Instantly feeling completely out of place, I said, "I'm just a guy who talked to your dad a couple of days ago about Jesus and the importance of church. And, your dad was actually excited about coming back to the Catholic Church. Whether you're guilty or not, that's not my business, but there's a priest who serves here as a chaplain, and he is available to meet with you, if you'd like. Your father told me you were raised Catholic, so please go see the priest, talk to him, and he'll keep everything you discuss completely confidential. Your dad wanted to invite you back to Jesus and his Church, because he just made the decision to return himself."

Saint Thomas Aquinas wrote, "To convert somebody go and take them by the hand and guide them." That's what I did in the county jail. I felt that I did what Michael wanted me to do. I invited his son, Keith, to come home to God and the Church.

Tracey, Keith, and his sister spoke together for about fifteen minutes, then the guard escorted Keith back to his cell, and we left the county jail.

Two days later I went to Michael's wake and took a seat in the back of the room. A number of family members and friends, all strangers to me, came to pay their respects to Michael. After half an hour, a priest arrived; he read some short prayers, then said a few words of consolation to the family. As the wake ended, I realized that Tracey hadn't shown up, and I hoped that perhaps she would meet us at the cemetery.

At the cemetery, as I walked to the grave with Michael's family and friends, I looked around for Tracey, but she was not there. Michael's casket lay beneath a broad black canopy. With the holy water in one hand and the Sacramentary in the other, I began to read the committal prayers, just as Father Doug had taught me a couple days before. Then it was time for Michael's eulogy. Although I had never met him in person, the family had asked me to deliver the eulogy as well. I had decided to base the eulogy on Michael's decision to return to the Church. I said, "I think the message that Michael would want all of you to know is that God has a wonderful plan for each of your lives. Michael would want to encourage you to come home to the Church, just like he was planning to do." As the graveside service ended and everyone walked to their cars to drive to the reception, Heather and I were the last ones to leave. As she said a final goodbye to her dad, Tracey finally arrived. She jumped out of her dented van, crying uncontrollably. "I missed everything! I missed Michael's funeral. I was in a wreck," Tracey said. It seemed to me that circumstances had come full circle: Tracey first helped others; now she was in need of consolation and support.

Later that weekend, I reflected back on everything that had occurred since my breakfast with Tracey: her entrance into the Church, my phone conversation with Michael, the visit to help Keith in jail, the graveside eulogy, and finally Tracey's accident. "Life with God is certainly unpredictable," I thought.

Life is a mystery, like that iceberg I mentioned earlier in this chapter. We can never be certain what lies beneath the surface of our day-to-day experiences. So many plans don't go as expected, and life gets complicated. Yet, with God we have purpose, and our faith gives us hope. With God all things are truly possible. When we follow the promptings of the Holy Spirit, we are sometimes invited to share his love with others, sometimes many others, in the mission of helping Catholics come home.

Today and every day, Our Lord calls upon you and me to use our specific talents, in our particular occupations and neighborhoods, to serve him by living and sharing our faith with those around us. Today so much emphasis is placed on making decisions based on our feelings, on not going beyond our comfort zone. But doing something that is necessary, even if it may be uncomfortable, not only builds character; it also strengthens our faith and helps us to grow in fortitude. Pushing beyond your comfort zone is an act of trust in the Holy Spirit, and it is an opportunity to tap into some of your hidden potential. Remember, just a single moment of encounter may be all it takes to change a soul.

Father Lawrence Lovasik teaches: "Kindness is constantly winning stray souls back to God by opening hearts that seemed obstinately closed. Kindness converted more sinners than either zeal, eloquence, or learning; and these three last have never converted anyone, unless they were kind also."

We make our Lord known through the example of our life, looking for occasions to speak out, not missing a single opportunity. Our task consists to a large extent in making the way to Christ cheerful and attractive. If we behave like that, many will be encouraged to follow it and to bring the joy and peace of the Lord to other men and women.

Francis Fernandez, In Conversation with God

Thoughts for Reflection

When someone asks you to pray for them or for someone in need, pray right then on the spot! Not only does this help them with an immediate prayer, but it also helps you in some mysterious way to remember to pray for them later.

When you encounter people who tell you their problems and the worries in their lives, have the courage to ask them, "How can I pray for you?" Oftentimes, they have a big burden they are carrying, and your offer to pray for them will show them love and compassion. Oh, and don't forget to pray for them!

CHAPTER 8

Ask, Seek, Knock

Declare his glory among the nations,
his marvelous works among all the peoples!

1 CHRONICLES 16:24

So many people are in such great need of love. The Jewish phi-
losopher Philo of Alexandria (ca. 20 BC–ca. AD 40) said, "Be
kind, for everyone you meet is fighting a great battle." He knew
that people were hurting. In spite of appearances, in spite of the
face we show to the world, each one of us is wounded. Too many
of us try to soothe our wounds with the "remedies" the world suggests: materialism, entertainment, hobbies, sex, food, drink, drugs.
Instead of making us feel better, these things often distract us
from God and, consequently, leave us feeling unloved and empty.
No matter what challenges you and your family may be facing
— unemployment, financial worries, health problems, addictions,
divorce — the only source of lasting hope, comfort, and security
is Almighty God.

The early Christians were so caring and compassionate that
their pagan neighbors marveled, "See how [these Christians] love
one another." Even though Christianity was outlawed for the first
three hundred years, the Church flourished and grew. The loving
kindness of the first Christians attracted converts and built up the
Church. It is no different today; everyone wants to be surrounded

by loving, caring people.

It is through love that Jesus attracts souls to himself. It is out of love that Jesus rescues lost sheep. Furthermore, Christ expects each baptized Christian to join in his soul-saving mission.

Before ascending into heaven, Jesus said, "Go therefore and make disciples of all nations" (Mt 28:19). Ever since, the Catholic Church has understood that its primary mission is evangelization. But evangelization is not limited to missionaries in far-off lands. You and I have a mission to carry the message of the Gospel and the love of God to our family and friends, neighbors and coworkers. But God doesn't force us; he gives us free will, so we need to be open to allowing God to use us, and ask him for this blessing.

Jesus promised us, "Ask, and it will be given you; seek, and you will find; knock, and it will be opened to you. For every one who asks receives, and he who seeks finds, and to him who knocks it will be opened" (Mt 7:7–8). Don't be shy about asking someone if they would like to return to the Faith. Don't be afraid to seek out the lost sheep. Trust that Our Lord is already knocking on the door of their heart; your invitation may be the final push they need to open the door and let Christ in.

Perhaps you're thinking, "My faith is private. I don't want to *proselytize*." Perhaps you are afraid that you don't know the Faith well enough to explain it to others. But you do not have to be a theologian. What you are doing is planting the seed, and you do that not by tackling difficult doctrinal questions, but by telling your own story of the good things God has done in your life. You can talk about the prayers that God has answered, the peace that was restored in your family, and all the other blessings that God has given to you. If you speak from the heart, if you speak sincerely and with love, wonderful things can happen, even in a single moment. Don't be afraid. Be open and pray every day that God will grant you the grace to help lead someone to Christ. So many lay apostles are already answering this call, as are many parishes, countless priests and deacons, religious sisters, and bishops who courageously and lovingly work together as a family to bring our brothers and sisters home. In 2006, on the fortieth anniversary of the publication of the Vatican II document *Ad Gentes*, Pope Benedict XVI reminded the Church that evangelization "is not something optional, but the very vocation of the People of God, a duty that corresponds to it by the command of the Lord Jesus Christ himself."

Before you begin speaking of the Faith, listen to the person you're about to address. What struggles or challenges are they facing? Has your friend just gone through a significant loss? Your effort with them will be in vain if you spend an hour telling your friend about the intricacies of Marian doctrine, when what they really need to hear is the Church's restorative teaching on redemptive suffering. All too often, we resort to intellectual defenses for the Catholic Faith when someone is struggling with a deep emotional setback that needs to be addressed altogether differently — yet with the truth of the Church. Remember, nobody cares how much you know until they know how much you care. This is worth repeating: Nobody cares how much you know until they know how much you care. Don't just talk in a God-loving way. Be and exist in a God-loving way. And keep the words to a minimum.

We are all called, each in our way, to guide souls. We have to be open to the Holy Spirit and seize God's gift of opportunity. In the words of Saint Paul in 1 Corinthians 9:16, "Woe to me if I do not preach the gospel!" When the Holy Spirit gives you the opportunity to talk to someone about the Faith, don't turn away. And when you give your testimony, do so with humility and compassion, not with judgment and condemnation.

Jesus didn't come to condemn the world; He came to save it. "For God so loved the world that he gave his only Son, that whoever believes in him should not perish but have eternal life. For God sent the Son into the world, not to condemn the world, but that the world might be saved through him" (Jn 3:16–17). Have you ever heard better news? Remember, no matter what you have done, it's never too late to accept God's love, mercy, and forgiveness. We serve a God who offers us unlimited do-overs through the divine mercy of Jesus. Jesus' mercy is a free gift placed in front of each of us. All we have to do is accept it.

Every day, all day long, God is saying to you, "I'm here. I love you. Return to me." Most people who do not hear God's invitation are not actively rejecting him; they are so absorbed in the distractions of the world that they are barely aware that God exists. Nonetheless, the gift of his mercy is always available, waiting for the day when those lost sheep realize how much they need it.

If members of your family are among those lost sheep who have drifted away from the Church, never stop praying for them. One of the most efficacious moments to pray for their return comes at Mass, when the priest raises the chalice of the Precious Blood of Jesus during the consecration. Remember that out of love and compassion for sinful humankind, Christ poured out his blood for the salvation of the world. He does not want to lose a single soul. So at the elevation of the chalice, mention the names of your loved ones, put them into the Precious Blood of Jesus, and ask the Lord to bring them home.

Perhaps the greatest spiritual challenge our families face today is the battle against secular humanism. Secular humanism is defined as "humanistic philosophy viewed as a non-theistic religion antagonistic to traditional religion." Another source says that it is "a religious worldview based on atheism, naturalism, evolution, and ethical relativism," and that secular humanists are atheists who adopt "ethical relativism" — the idea that there is no absolute moral code, so we're free to adjust our ethical standards to suit each situation.

This sinister philosophy makes almost no demands. It promotes ideas that, on the surface at least, appear attractive. Cultural elites such as commentators in the media, those in some areas of academia, and many in Hollywood tell us that this philosophy is what the intelligent, trendy people believe. It is seductive, this idea that there are no absolutes of right and wrong, that morality is one big gray area, so everyone should live in a manner that is most comfortable for them. Even religious believers can find secular humanism hard to resist, as I knew all too well. But you must resist it. This is not the Gospel; this is not God's plan for humankind. If you find yourself too caught up in the *busyness* of your daily routine, if you find yourself missing Mass and skipping your prayers, then slam on the brakes and look around — not just outwardly, but inwardly. Is there a void? If so, then Mass, frequent reception of the sacraments, and private prayer are the keys to abiding in God's peace and recognizing your true purpose in this world. While it's important to love others to heaven, it's equally important to love ourselves to heaven as well, and we do this by resting in the presence of the Lord.

Do you recall the story of Jesus' visit to the home of the two sisters, Mary and Martha (Lk 10:38–42)? While Martha bustled about seeing to the meal and the table so that everything would be perfect for her guest, Mary sat at the feet of Jesus, listening to every word he said, nurturing her spiritual life. At the end of this episode, Jesus reminds us: "Mary has chosen the good portion, which shall not be taken away from her" (Lk 10:42). As lay Christians, we need to have a finely tuned mix of both the contemplative and the active life. First, we need to be filled with God's word in Scripture, grace from the sacraments, and the peace and wisdom that come from contemplative prayer. Only then will we be more fully equipped to faithfully and productively carry out our active apostolic mission, guided by the Holy Spirit. We must be filled up by means of contemplative prayer, then be active when we need to be active.

In his book *The Soul of the Apostolate*, Dom Jean-Baptiste Chautard, a French Cistercian abbot, refers to this scene in the house of Mary and Martha when he writes about people who love action for action's sake:

> Any pretext will serve if we can only escape this discipline
> of our faculties: business, family problems, health, good
> reputation, patriotism, the honor of one's congregation,
> and the pretend glory of God, all vie with one another in

preventing us from living within ourselves. This sort of frenzy for exterior life finally succeeds in gaining over us an attraction that we can no longer resist. Is there any reason to be surprised, then, that the interior life is neglected?

Dom Chautard says that we can overlook the value of "living with Christ, in Christ and through Christ, and of forgetting that everything, in the plan of Redemption, is based on the Eucharistic life as much as it is upon the rock of Peter." He urges us, even during the busiest days, to slip away for a few minutes and "go and purify and rekindle [your] energy before the Tabernacle ... to obtain from its Divine Guest better results for [your] work."

Accept the gift of God's mercy. Let yourself be filled with the graces of the Holy Spirit, so that the light of Christ and the love of our heavenly Father can overflow through you to those you meet. The time is now!

> *As each has received a gift, employ it for one another,*
> *as good stewards of God's varied grace.*
> 1 PETER 4:10

Maybe you will also be surprised to learn that God gives us a promised reward for those who share the Good News of Jesus. It's in James 5:19–20. "My brethren, if any one among you wanders from the truth and some one brings him back, let him know that whoever brings back a sinner from the error of his way will save his soul from death and will cover a multitude of sins." When we ask, seek, and know, our loving Father offers each one of us the incredible opportunity to invite souls close to him — sometimes in a single moment.

Thoughts for Reflection

When speaking with someone who is struggling with the Church's discipline or moral teachings, try a personalized version of the "feel, felt, found" technique. Here's how it goes: "With regard to Jesus' teachings on [the sanctity of life, contraception, traditional marriage, going to a priest for confession], I know how you feel. In fact, I [and many people I know] felt the same way at one time. But after studying the *Catechism of the Catholic Church*, I found that Jesus' teaching on that subject makes perfect sense. Here's why ..."

This feel, felt, found technique allows you to be empathetic without being confrontational about the person's point of view. It is a gentle way to share the truth and guide the conversation to a more positive outcome. In doing this you take another step toward loving someone to heaven.

CHAPTER 9

Never Give Up

So, being affectionately desirous of you, we were ready to share with you not only the gospel of God but also our own selves, because you had become very dear to us.

1 THESSALONIANS 2:8

My family lived in Phoenix, Arizona, for thirty-six years, where we heard the legend of an old desert prospector who spent years chipping away inside a mountain cave, certain that at any moment he would strike gold. After years of digging, he finally gave up and abandoned his claim. Then another old prospector came along, bought the claim, and started digging. He had dug only one foot into the rock when he discovered the largest gold deposit in Arizona history. These prospectors teach us a clear lesson: We must never give up.

Saint Paul teaches us to persevere, to keep our eyes on Christ and never lose hope, no matter how difficult or discouraging our journey may become. And he urges us always to be ready to carry the Good News announced by Jesus Christ to our neighbors, "in season and out of season" (2 Tm 4:2).

Not long ago, I took an early morning flight from Wichita to Atlanta. Getting up while it was still dark was hard, but I consoled myself with the thought that at least I'd be comfortable on the plane; I had received an upgrade to first class, thanks to being a frequent flier. Unfortunately, after boarding the plane, I found that we had been assigned an old aircraft that did not have a first-class section. Some of the first-class passengers lost their temper and took out their frustrations on the flight crew.

Thankfully, I kept my cool this day. After all, it wasn't the flight attendants' fault, and they were doing their best to make everyone comfortable. So, when one of the flight attendants brought me a cup of coffee, I said to her, "You know, even though we don't have a first-class section today, you're still giving all of us first-class service. Thank you so much." This flight attendant wore a name badge that read "Jessie." She smiled and said, "Thank you so much for saying that. It's been a tough morning and a rough week in general." We talked a little bit more, and then she moved on to serve the other passengers.

We were about halfway through our flight when I saw Jessie talking with another flight attendant. They were whispering, so I could not hear what they were saying, but from her tone of voice it was obvious that Jessie was distraught. I prayed and wondered what I could do to help her. After that prayer, I felt led to take out a Catholics Come Home evangelization card from my wallet and to write on the back of it: "Jessie, the hope that you seek comes only from Jesus and his Church. God loves you! Tom."

At the end of the flight, as the crew prepared for landing, Jessie came down the aisle one last time. As she was passing my seat, she stopped and said, "I can't thank you enough for being so nice. I just really feel that we were supposed to meet you. Thank you so much." Handing her the card with the message, I said, "Please read this when you get off the plane."

About a week later, a letter arrived from Jessie. She wrote:

My name is Jessie. You were on my flight, and you handed me a card with a note on the back. How did you know I was so desperately in need of that message? I want to thank you. I have not stopped crying since I read your note and went to your website. I was raised Catholic, but had been away from the Church and God for many years. I'm recently divorced and struggling with the emptiness of being alone. I have been searching for a man to be in my life, and I have found that man. It's God.

Jessie had gone back to Mass and came home to God that past weekend. We sent Jessie a note of encouragement and urged her to keep on this new path of faith.

A few weeks after her first letter, Jessie wrote again, saying:

I've been feeling better lately. Praying a lot and vowing to be a good Christian. I'm making an effort to be a positive effect on at least one person every day. Yesterday I finished my last flight of the day after working twelve hours. My fellow crew members went home, while I stayed and helped a pregnant lady with three toddlers, a cat, a stroller, and six carry-on bags get to her next gate on time. It got me home about an hour late, but it felt good to help somebody in need.

See how love creates a ripple effect? When we share God's love with someone, often they will pass it on, changing our world for the better. It is God's plan for us to share the love of Christ every chance we get.

Ask yourself, "Am I letting Jesus fill me with his grace so that his grace can overflow into others through me?" If not, do all that you can to align yourself with his holy will. The way to begin is with the Sacrament of Reconciliation, then add more prayer, Eucharistic adoration, reading of the Bible and holy Catholic books, and spiritual direction. God our Father has given each of us particular talents and abilities. Each of us has a specific purpose in life. Every soul is called to a unique mission that only he or she can fulfill. This is our Father's amazing plan for each one of his children, intricately designed so that all of us who cooperate with his will can be happy in this life, and supremely happy with him forever in heaven.

Jesus is asking you now to tell others about our Father's love. Are you ready to join the New Evangelization? Are you willing to serve in the irreplaceable role that only you can fulfill? Are you prepared to help invite souls — especially the nearly one billion who were baptized Catholic but no longer practice their faith — into the largest family reunion in salvation history?

There's a popular Christian song on the radio by Martina McBride called "Do It Anyway," in which we are reminded that even when we don't feel like we have the time, energy, or talent, we should always do what's right and what God would want us to do at that moment. She urges us to step beyond convenience, comfort, and fear of embarrassment to "do it anyway," because serving God and others is how Christianity calls us to live every moment.

If you are still reluctant to share your gift of faith, be not afraid! After all, you are a child of God and a friend of Jesus. As Saint Teresa of Ávila once said, "All my longing was and still is that since [God] has so many enemies and so few friends, that these few friends be good ones."

Francis Fernandez, in his series of books *In Conversation with God*, encourages us to plunge deeper into our faith and be more committed in our service to others. "We have to show everyone that Christ is still alive," Fernandez writes, "by living heroically the events of our daily lives."

Gandhi put it more bluntly when he said, "Oh, I don't reject Christ. I love Christ. It's just that so many of you Christians are so *unlike* Christ. If Christians would really live according to the teachings of Christ, as found in the Bible, all of India would be Christian today."

So how can we be and live more like Christ? By surrendering completely to him! Let me explain. You've likely heard the saying, "Less is more." Well, that is often true spiritually as well, when we give our will to God and allow him to mold us into the likeness of Jesus. We do this by trusting in his divine providence and allowing Jesus to increase in our lives while we decrease.

For a minute, reflect in your mind on the Divine Mercy image of Jesus. It's the image of Jesus with rays of blood and water streaming from his heart. It was brought to the world by Saint Faustina, a Polish hero of the Faith. At the bottom of the Divine Mercy painting of Jesus, we see the words, *"Jezu Ufam Tobie,"* which translates into "Jesus, I trust in You." So how can we learn to trust in Jesus more, and rely on our own human ambitions and understanding less? With our evangelization efforts and prayers, and complete surrender to God's timing and perfect will, we will better understand that the Good Shepherd doesn't want to ever leave any soul behind. Jesus doesn't need us to bring souls home, but he wants us to help invite others in a cooperative manner. Grace builds on nature, and the Divine works through our humanity. God invites us to be part of his salvific mission.

A great way to begin surrendering to God's perfect will for your life is by praying the Surrender Novena by Father Don Dolindo Ruotolo, who lived from 1882 to 1970.

Novena of Surrender to the Will of God†
(Father Don Dolindo Ruotolo)

Day 1
Why do you confuse yourselves by worrying?
Leave the care of your affairs to me
and everything will be peaceful.
I say to you in truth that every act of true,
blind, complete surrender to me
produces the effect that you desire
and resolves all difficult situations.

(Repeat the following prayer ten times.)

---

† "Surrender Prayer" by Don Dolindo, trans. Giovanna Ellis. English translation © Giovanna Ellis, used with permission.

O Jesus, I surrender myself to you,
take care of everything!

_____

Day 2
Surrender to me does not mean to fret,
to be upset, or to lose hope,
nor does it mean offering to me a worried prayer
asking me to follow you
and change your worry into prayer.
It is against this surrender,
deeply against it, to worry,
to be nervous
and to desire to think about the consequences of anything.
It is like the confusion that children feel
when they ask their mother to see to their needs,
and then try to take care of those needs for themselves
so that their childlike efforts get in their mother's way.
Surrender means to placidly close the eyes of the soul,
to turn away from thoughts of tribulation
and to put yourself in my care, so that only I act,
saying You take care of it.

(Repeat the following prayer ten times.)

O Jesus, I surrender myself to you,
take care of everything!

_____

Day 3
How many things I do when the soul,
in so much spiritual and material need turns to me,
looks at me and says to me;
"You take care of it,"
then closes its eyes and rests.

In pain you pray for me to act,
but that I act in the way you want.
You do not turn to me, instead,
you want me to adapt to your ideas.
You are not sick people who ask the doctor to cure you,
but rather sick people who tell the doctor how to.
So do not act this way,
but pray as I taught you in the Our Father:
"Hallowed be thy Name,"
that is, be glorified in my need.
"Thy kingdom come,"
that is, let all that is in us
and in the world be in accord with your kingdom.
"Thy will be done on Earth as it is in Heaven,"
that is, in our need,
decide as you see fit for our temporal and eternal life.
If you say to me truly:
"Thy will be done"
which is the same as saying:
"You take care of it"
I will intervene with all my omnipotence,
and I will resolve the most difficult situations.

(Repeat the following prayer ten times.)

O Jesus, I surrender myself to you,
take care of everything!

Day 4
You see evil growing instead of weakening?
Do not worry,
Close your eyes and say to me with faith:
"Thy will be done, You take care of it."
I say to you that I will take care of it,

and that I will intervene as does a doctor
and I will accomplish miracles when they are needed.
Do you see that the sick person is getting worse?
Do not be upset,
but close your eyes and say
"You take care of it."
I say to you that I will take care of it,
and that there is no medicine
more powerful than my loving intervention.
By my love, I promise this to you.

(Repeat the following prayer ten times.)

O Jesus, I surrender myself to you,
take care of everything!

_____

Day 5

And when I must lead you on a path different from the one you
see,
I will prepare you;
I will carry you in my arms;
I will let you find yourself,
like children who have fallen asleep in their mother's arms,
on the other bank of the river.
What troubles you and hurts you immensely are your reason,
your thoughts and worry,
and your desire at all costs to deal with what afflicts you.

(Repeat the following prayer ten times.)

O Jesus, I surrender myself to you,
take care of everything!

Day 6
You are sleepless;
you want to judge everything,
direct everything and see to everything
and you surrender to human strength,
or worse — to men themselves,
trusting in their intervention,
— this is what hinders my words and my views.
Oh how much I wish from you this surrender,
to help you and how I suffer when I see you so agitated!
Satan tries to do exactly this:
to agitate you and to remove you from my protection
and to throw you into the jaws of human initiative.
So, trust only in me,
rest in me,
surrender to me in everything.

(Repeat the following prayer ten times.)

O Jesus, I surrender myself to you,
take care of everything!

Day 7
I perform miracles in proportion to your full surrender to me
and to your not thinking of yourselves.
I sow treasure troves of graces
when you are in the deepest poverty.
No person of reason, no thinker,
has ever performed miracles,
not even among the saints.
He does divine works whosoever surrenders to God.
So don't think about it anymore,
because your mind is acute
and for you it is very hard to see evil

and to trust in me
and to not think of yourself.
Do this for all your needs,
do this all of you
and you will see great continual silent miracles.
I will take care of things,
I promise this to you.

(Repeat the following prayer ten times.)

O Jesus, I surrender myself to you,
take care of everything!

Day 8
Close your eyes and let yourself be carried away
on the flowing current of my grace;
close your eyes and do not think of the present,
turning your thoughts away from the future
just as you would from temptation.
Repose in me, believing in my goodness,
and I promise you by my love that if you say
"You take care of it," I will take care of it all;
I will console you,
liberate you and guide you.

(Repeat the following prayer ten times.)

O Jesus, I surrender myself to you,
take care of everything!

Day 9
Pray always in readiness to surrender,
and you will receive from it great peace and great rewards,

even when I confer on you the grace of immolation,
of repentance and of love.
Then what does suffering matter?
It seems impossible to you?
Close your eyes and say with all your soul,
"Jesus, you take care of it."
Do not be afraid, I will take care of things
and you will bless my name by humbling yourself.
A thousand prayers cannot equal one single act of surrender,
remember this well.
There is no novena more effective than this:

(Repeat the following prayer ten times.)

O Jesus, I surrender myself to you,
take care of everything!

Mother, I am yours now and forever.
Through you and with you
I always want to belong completely to Jesus.

———————

Tens of thousands of people have found great peace and hope when
praying this novena and trusting God. Who doesn't need more
peace, when the attacks of the world and the evil one are constantly trying to prevent us from our Christian mission as the Church
Militant on earth?

So, let's bring Christ's compassion to the wounded souls around
us. Let us take the Blessed Mother as our role model, imitating her
by trying to serve the Lord with our entire heart and will. Let's look
to her as the perfect example of evangelization, humility, obedience,
and surrender. Mary is the living monstrance who holds up Jesus for
all the world to see.

We must do the same by bringing the light of the Eucharistic

Christ to a hurting world in need of great hope. God is calling you to help Catholics come home. How will you answer him? If you and I don't share the Faith, Catholicism could become the greatest story *never* told.

A new dawn is shining on our world today. A fresh springtime of hope awaits us! God is calling little souls like you and me to take part in big adventures. All it takes is a simple moment of encounter to join this mission of the New Evangelization and help love somebody to heaven!

Come and see what God has done: he is terrible in his deeds among men.

PSALM 66:5

Thoughts for Reflection

When someone questions your desire to help souls home to the Catholic Church and questions you with, "What are they coming home to?" answer as follows: "They are coming home to the Church founded over two thousand years ago by Jesus himself. Through his Church, Jesus feeds us with his own Body and Blood in the Eucharist, and forgives us through the Sacrament of Confession. And in spite of all our human frailties and failings, Jesus has promised us that the Holy Spirit will guide his Church, and that it will endure until the end of time. There is no alternative, no second best."

CHAPTER 10

For Such a Time as This

Let him know that whoever brings back a sinner from the error of his way will save his soul from death and will cover a multitude of sins.

JAMES 5:20

Over the past twenty-three years at Catholics Come Home, we've heard from some of the hundreds of thousands of people who have returned to the Catholic Church or converted to the Faith thanks to God's grace working through our apostolate. Some of these people are featured on our popular prime-time television series called *Catholics Come Home*, which airs worldwide on EWTN, an international Catholic television network started by Mother Angelica.

We praise God that, as of this writing, we are in our sixth season on EWTN, having featured about seventy testimonial interviews with people who are now close to the Lord — former atheists, agnostics, or fallen-away Catholics who are all now passionate disciples of Christ.

Dr. Gloria Sampson, a PhD in linguistics, was raised Catholic, but fell away in college and was an atheist for more than fifty years. She taught communists in China how to speak English during the Cold War days of the 1950s and '60s. After a divorce, she thought, "I've been without God for so long, I guess I don't need God."

Dr. Sampson in Vancouver, British Columbia.

One night, as she shared in the premiere episode of *Catholics Come Home* on EWTN, she saw a "very unusual ad. It said 'Catholics Come Home.' I'd never heard it that way: Come home!" She visited the website to learn more, and through the draw of the Holy Spirit realized that she still believed after fifty-three years! She was then invited by a neighbor to a parish faith gathering of people from many backgrounds with various testimonies.

"I know God exists. I searched for the truth as an academic all my life, but there was one truth I was missing — and that was God. When we sing the Our Father, that is the most beautiful thing in the world. I have no will of my own left. It's all God's will, the way it should be. All I want to do now is evangelize!"

Michael Mark, a Chinese man raised in Philadelphia's Chinatown, shared his conversion on a *Catholics Come Home* episode, too. "I lived a life of drugs, sex, stealing. It really strained not only my relationship with my dad, but with God. I got clean ... but something was missing. While watching TV, I witnessed a Catholics Come Home *evangomercial*™ testimony from a Catholic who had a similar situation. ... I went to Mass and ... I was welcomed with open arms! When I started going to church, my ninety-year-old dad, who also had stopped practicing his faith, would accompany me, and it was such a blessing ... like the Parable of the Prodigal Son."

Michael and his ninety-year-old father returned to the Church in Philadelphia's Chinatown. Now, Michael serves at the homeless shelter and hospice, helping dying men on the streets of downtown. Michael is like a "Mother Teresa" to his community!

He added, "The last week I was with my dad … he told me he loved me … and, like God the Father, has forgiven me. I owe CCH a sincere thank you for helping me come home."

Raised Buddhist, Daniel Bui immigrated to America and later attended a Christian church with his parents. But he wondered about Christ's hope for Christian unity and differing beliefs on the Eucharist. He came upon a pamphlet, "How to Stay Christian in College," and contacted the author, who introduced him to natural law and the early Church Fathers. He read Benedict XVI's *Jesus of Nazareth*, "and the first chapter just blew me away," he said. A young practicing Catholic acquaintance then shared a Catholics Come Home evangomercial and the website

Daniel Bui in Austin, Texas

with him. All these promptings helped lead him to an RCIA program. Daniel is now an active Catholic, discerning the priesthood. Daniel says, "Life is a lot deeper now."

Raised in a culturally Jewish family, Beth Kuklinski suffered a tough childhood. With no faith, she became depressed. After a divorce, she sought counseling and tried medication, but nothing really helped. Then "I saw a CCH evangomercial, and couldn't get it out of my head! I started going to Mass and was attracted to the Eucharist even before I became Catholic. I wanted to be in a loving place and work toward eternal life. I became Catholic and sat for forty minutes in my first confession. It was a wonderful experience. I'm a changed person! God is a loving God, and he asks us to share that love with our neighbor."

Another CCH episode features business executive Tom Henderson, who was a self-proclaimed agnostic. "I thought I could take care of myself," Henderson said. He soon saw a CCH evangomercial, and he testified: "I learned from that commercial — that with the guidance of the Holy Spirit, the Church had compiled the Bible long ago. ... The need for authority became self-evident to me." Henderson discovered that faith and reason exist together in the Church: "Jesus delivered a hard teaching around the Body and Blood of Christ. I'd never heard the part in John 6 before, and so clearly: This was a hard teaching, and many turned away — but Jesus didn't stop them. The Catholic Church has this exact teaching on the Eucharist." Henderson later joined RCIA and now, as a practicing Catholic, attends Mass with his wife.

Thomas Manns shared his incredible journey home on a *Catholics Come Home* episode, too. He lived for years as an agnostic, but a traumatic injury and disease left him depressed. "I cursed God for keeping me alive. Satan wanted me to think about suicide. Then I saw a Catholics Come Home commercial. Something snapped. I then read the book, *Catholics Come Home: God's Extraordinary Plan for Your Life*. So many points were just dead-on! I walked into a church and thought, 'This is where I'm supposed to be. This is home.' Coming back to the Church is the first step to healing; I went from being desperate to finding hope. Catholics Come Home helped save my life and take the path [God] planned."

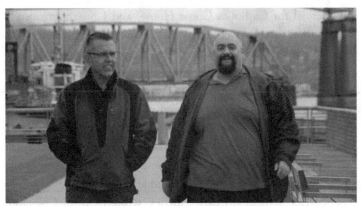

Former hermit, Thomas Manns (right), lives in Canada.

Guest and convert Remington Stewart shared another journey. Remi "didn't think it was possible to have a relationship with God." He became involved with pornography, and soon after also lost someone he loved. "What did it mean to 'come home?' I didn't know the Catholic Church goes back to the beginning," he said. He watched every CCH episode, attracted by the mercy of Jesus Christ. "Who wouldn't want to ask for it? Lord Jesus Christ, have mercy on me, a sinner."

Other stories of people who contacted us after coming home to their Catholic roots or converting include one young man who left the Church and became a Muslim in his twenties; he returned to his Catholic faith after seeing a Catholics Come Home evangomercial on television in Boston.

We also learned about a young Polish immigrant in Chicago who had drifted into agnosticism during his teenage years, until he saw a Catholics Come Home ad on Polsat, the Polish language television station. He came home, too.

A middle-aged Irish woman named Maggie wrote to us telling about how she came back to the Church after being away for decades, saying: "I moved to Northern Arizona from Dublin, Ireland, thirty years ago, and I gave up my faith. And for a while I wasn't going to church anymore. Soon, I became an agnostic. I didn't even know if there was a God, or care. But then I saw the commercial for Catholics Come Home, and I began to weep. I went online to your website [www.catholicscomehome.org] and looked up my parish Mass times. And I came home after all these years." I e-mailed Maggie and started asking her a few questions, having been intrigued by her story. Maggie told me that her mother back in Dublin had never stopped praying for her return to the Faith — just as Saint Monica had prayed for her son Augustine. Through God's grace and her mother's prayers, the Holy Spirit orchestrated the Catholics Come Home television ad to air at the right time to touch Maggie's heart and lead her home.

Scott, a man in his early thirties, wrote us from Colorado: "I was born Catholic, but I drifted and became an atheist. For years I called myself an atheist and said religion was irrelevant. I came across the [www.catholicscomehome.org] website, looked at the ads and thought that it kind of makes some sense. And I started investigating it some more." That Easter, Scott returned to the Catholic Church. Later, we learned that Scott was evangelizing his brother, who professed to be an atheist. Scott was helping to invite his brother home, too. When one soul helps another soul, countless souls can be helped.

Next there is Henry, a college student at an interdenominational university in Tulsa. Henry was a faithful Protestant, but felt that there was something missing in his spiritual life. Henry admitted that over the last few years, he had started investigating other faiths. He said, "I stumbled upon Catholics Come Home and our [www.catolicosregresen.org] Spanish website and started looking into Catholic teachings." Today, not only is Henry a practicing Catholic, but he also completed a master's program in theology at a Catholic university and is now teaching the Faith.

When we hear these stories, we see how God's grace blesses humanity. These are "God-incidences," where God is directly touching the lives of people, then using them to bring others to the fullness of faith. God wants you and me to do the same.

After airing Catholics Come Home evangelization campaigns in more than forty archdioceses and dioceses, and more recently in nine foreign languages across the world, we've received very encouraging and interesting reports from our diocesan partners. Most noted sizable increases in Mass attendance and participation in the Sacrament of Reconciliation. Many dioceses reported a rise in volunteerism and tithing, because current Catholics felt a renewed sense of pride in their Church and stronger Catholic identity. Countless parishes cited an increase in RCIA inquiries from people who had seen the *evangomercials*™. A number of parish priests and diocesan officials claim that most of the returnees they have spoken with didn't have serious reasons for leaving the Church; that most inactive Catholics don't hate the Church; and that most have not fallen completely away from God, either. Many admitted that they just drifted away because life got too busy, or they had to take their kids to sporting events on Sunday. About 10 percent of the returnees said that they were divorced and didn't know whether they could still be members of the Church — wondering whether they were excommunicated.

Cultural Trends That Affect Souls

More than sixty years ago, Archbishop Fulton J. Sheen encouraged us to go deeper into our faith. His TV program *Life Is Worth Living* was the number one show in the United States during the 1950s, with higher ratings than the variety show of legendary comedian Milton Berle. Archbishop Sheen said, "Really, most of us live below the level of our energy. And, in order to be happy, we need to do more. Now, we can do more spiritually and in every other way. So you see how important it is to have the mind to do all that you can do? To work to the limit of your ability. Our world is really suffering from indifference. Indifference is apathy, not caring."

Archbishop Sheen continues to challenge us to live our faith to the fullest, to aim for heaven, and to make a positive difference in the lives of others. Why? Because Jesus shows us the way, modeling mercy and compassion, even though as sinners we don't deserve his love. Christ calls us to take up our cross daily, to put aside our selfish ways, and to follow him. We must fight the indifference and apathy, overcome the noise and distractions that battle for our attention, our time, and our hearts. If we truly love Jesus, we will honor our Lord as he pleads with us to "feed my sheep."

Years ago, Father Henry Atem, originally from Cameroon, Africa, invited me to speak at the African Conference of Catho-

Tom speaking at ACCCRUS conference of African Clergy serving in America.

lic Clergy and Religious in the United States, held in Atlanta. It was an awesome experience, and the priests and religious sisters from Africa who are serving in America were so filled with joy and incredibly kind to me. During the question-and-answer session following my speech, one of the nuns stood up and said, "Americans came to evangelize us years ago; now we are coming back from Africa to help re-evangelize America today." I thank God for these faithful witnesses who have traveled so far from home, so far from family and the comfortable familiarity of their own homelands, and made the sacrifice to help lead souls back to Christ and his Church. When I asked these faithful witnesses the reason for their obvious joy, they replied, "Joy: Jesus, others, you. ... We must prioritize them in this order!"

The culture has changed considerably since the time when Fulton Sheen captured viewers' hearts. Having served as president of three advertising agencies, with a marketing and communications career spanning nearly thirty years, I've witnessed the power of media and how electronic communications dominate our lives. Recent studies confirm that Americans spend one-third of their waking hours consuming media. The Internet is increasingly becoming our main addiction. Yet television is still king, and it dominates our lives. The Kaiser Family Foundation reports that

Americans spend nearly thirty-eight hours each week watching television. In fact, the statistics show that by the time the average American reaches the age of seventy-five, he will have spent fourteen years of his life watching television, and four years of his life just watching television commercials. Now, the trend shows most time is spent on social media and digital entertainment, more than traditional TV. As a recovering media junkie, I'm as guilty as the next person, and certainly I can't throw any stones.

But the facts regarding how much time we are wasting speak loudly. In his book *Jesus-Shock*, Peter Kreeft writes, "Our culture has filled our heads, but emptied our hearts. It's stuffed our wallets but starved our wonder. It has fed our thirst for facts, but not for meaning or mystery. It produces nice people, not heroes." There are a number of nice people in the world, but our culture and our Church are starving for authentic Catholic heroes who will make a difference. We need saints in the world today. Seventy percent of the more than 1.2 billion Catholics worldwide, many of them victims of our aggressively secular society, are no longer practicing their faith. They need our prayers and our help.

The Moral Void

Today our world lives by two self-centered ideologies: What's in it for me? and What is the very least I can do? A 2010 Gallup Poll found a growing divide between Church teachings and what people are actually doing. Gallup reported on the following key moral issues:

- Having a baby outside of marriage: 54 percent found it morally acceptable; only 42 percent said it was immoral.
- Same-sex relations: 52 percent said it was morally acceptable; only 43 percent said it was immoral.
- The death penalty: 65 percent said it was morally acceptable; only 26 percent said it was immoral.
- Assisted suicide: 49 percent said it was morally acceptable; only 44 percent said it was immoral.

Convert Lydia Clarke in Providence, Rhode Island.

These statistics should not evoke judgment; instead, they should remind us of the vital need to evangelize. The old saying, "Love the sinner, but hate the sin," still applies here. Who would want to come back to the Church if they thought that it condemns people? When sharing Jesus' teachings, we must always speak the truth with love in order to bring more souls to Christ. So as evangelists, let's remember Jesus' teaching of looking at the log in our own eye first before we see the splinter in our neighbor's eye. This will help us to approach people with more humility, love, and mercy, as Christ exemplified.

Every decade, more souls are being desensitized, negatively catechized by moral relativism and secular humanism. With each passing year, more souls veer further from the straight and narrow path that leads to eternal life. Eventually, additional souls will abandon the moral compass that, at one time, pointed them in the direction of Truth. At the farthest end of this spectrum from belief in God is atheism, and it is also on the rise in our culture. My dear friend and Catholic author Patrick Madrid, along with Kenneth Hensley, his coauthor, discusses the fallacies of atheism in his timely book *The Godless Delusion*. In large metropolitan areas such as Toronto, Seattle, and Chicago, atheists sponsor billboards and bus ads spreading godless propaganda to our youth and the culture at large. A few examples of their messages include, "There is probably no God ... so stop worrying and start living!" Another encourages: "Go ahead, sleep in on Sunday."

As a former advertising agency executive, I'm perplexed by this. I fail to understand the atheists' economic model. In other words, if atheists don't believe in God, why would they spend their hard-earned money to convince other people not to believe in him? You would think they would say, "You do your thing, and I'll do mine." But this isn't what they're doing. I fervently believe Saint Paul was right when he wrote in his Epistle to the Ephesians: "For we are not contending against flesh and blood, but against the principalities, against the powers, against the world rulers of this present darkness, against the spiritual hosts of wickedness in the heavenly places" (Eph 6:12). In the spiritual war, we must choose sides, either serving God and putting our complete hope and trust in the saving grace of Jesus, or choosing the dark way of the world. The atheists' advertising campaign shows their hand; it reveals their true motive — they are trying to lure souls away from God. The sinister forces of evil are at work in those billboards.

At this time in salvation history, Jesus is calling each one of us to pick sides and choose our path. We are called no longer to live in secular mediocrity, for we must submit to God's perfect will and aim for heaven. As faithful Catholics, we cannot live any longer in the mushy middle, in that lukewarm gray area. The time has come for us to live and serve heroically and reject the shades of gray. Our world is spiraling out of control, and too many people are becoming untethered from God. Now, more than ever, is our time to join the chorus of the saints in saying, "As for me and my house, we will serve the Lord" (Jos 24:15). Now is our time to answer Jesus' call to help rescue drifting souls, to help Catholics Come Home.

Thoughts for Reflection

*When you think of the poor who die of hunger, of victims
of catastrophes and of murderous wars, your heart breaks and your
pocketbook opens. And still more, your heart must break when you
think that souls are dying by the millions of spiritual hunger.
Jesus thirsts for these souls but they cannot go to Him, because
they do not know Him.*

JEAN C. J. D'ELBÉE, I BELIEVE IN LOVE

Appendix

T wo thousand years ago, Saint Paul advised the Christians in Ephesus, "Put on the whole armor of God, that you may be able to stand against the wiles of the devil" (Eph 6:11). If Saint Paul were writing today, he might replace the term "armor" with "tool kit." That is what is assembled for you here — your complete Catholic Evangelization Tool Kit. I've listed my favorite books, which I hope will increase your faith in God and your devotion to the Blessed Mother and the saints. I've assembled a handful of my favorite Catholic quotations, which inspire me in my work of evangelization. I've collected my favorite prayers, both traditional and contemporary, that soothe my heart and mind, and feed my soul. I know that these prayers will help you to stay connected to the Holy Trinity and all the saints in heaven. I've also included a short listing of some of my favorite Catholic groups that have blessed my life. And finally, as you prepare to bring Catholics home, I will close my book the way Archbishop Fulton Sheen, the greatest American evangelist of all time, always wrapped up his television program: "God love you!"

SUGGESTED READING FOR ASPIRING CATHOLIC EVANGELISTS

The WillPower Advantage: Building Habits for Lasting Happiness, by **Tom Peterson and Ryan Hanning, PhD, (San Francisco: Ignatius Press, 2020).**
My latest book leads each reader through a Spiritual Audit which

helps them more fully surrender to God's perfect Will and find lasting happiness.

***Epic! The Story of Jesus' Holy Catholic Church,* by Tom Peterson (Charlotte, NC: Tan Books/St Benedict Press, 2020).**
This is an illustrated book featuring the history, beauty, spirituality, and accomplishments of our Catholic family.

***Trustful Surrender to Divine Providence: The Secret of Peace and Happiness,* by Jean Baptiste Saint-Jure, SJ, and Saint Claude de la Colombiere, SJ (Charlotte, NC: TAN Books, 1984).**
This has to be among my top ten favorite, life-changing books of all time. Trusting God helps reduce stress, eases the workload, and brings you in close relationship with your Father in heaven. Amazingly, I even learned that God allows all things that will occur; after all, he is God and could stop certain things from happening. But God brings good even out of the bad, for our sanctification and his glory.

***The Soul of the Apostolate,* by Dom Jean-Baptiste Chautard, OCSO (Charlotte, NC: TAN Books, 1977).**
This is a must-read book for anyone with a vocation or anyone who leads an apostolate (which means this book is pretty much for everyone!). Chautard is a wise mentor, and his writings are classic, feeding us with nutrient-rich spiritual wisdom to help in everyday situations.

***I Believe in Love: Retreat Conference on the Interior Life,* by Père Jean du Coeur de Jésus d'Elbée, trans. Marilyn Teichert (Petersham, MA: Saint Bede's Publications, 1983).**
A small book that brings the reader on a spiritual retreat led by the teachings of the Little Flower, Saint Thérèse of Lisieux. Jesus thirsts for souls, and d'Elbée shows us how to help bring more thirsting souls home to Jesus.

Head & Heart: Becoming Spiritual Leaders for your Family, by Katie Warner (Steubenville, OH: Emmaus Road, 2015).
This book helps men understand their role as head of the family, and women as heart of the family. A great book especially for young married couples. Check out all the books and resources for children, too, at www.katiewarner.com.

Reasons to Believe: How to Understand, Explain, and Defend the Catholic Faith, by Scott Hahn (New York: Doubleday, 2007).
This book is a great resource for learning the why's and how's of your Catholic faith. It is a powerful book to get into the hands of your fallen-away Catholic or non-Catholic friends and relatives, too. With all of these reasons to believe, it's hard not to be convinced by the truth of the Catholic Faith by the end of this book.

I'm Not Being Fed: Discovering the Food That Satisfies the Soul, by Jeff Cavins (West Chester, PA: Ascension Press, 2005).
Jeff Cavins has a gift for taking complex theological concepts and explaining them so that everyone understands. As a baptized Catholic who turned Protestant pastor, then reverted back to the Catholic Faith, Jeff is ideally suited to discuss why people leave the Faith, as well as ways to invite souls home to the Catholic Church.

Crossing the Tiber: Evangelical Protestants Discover the Historical Church, by Stephen Ray (San Francisco: Ignatius Press, 1997).
Steve Ray blesses audiences across the world with his knowledge of Scripture, history, and the Catholic Faith. As a convert, Steve brings a wealth of information that will help you share the Faith with neighbors.

***Rome Sweet Home: Our Journey to Catholicism,* by Scott and Kimberly Hahn (San Francisco: Ignatius Press, 1993).**
This is one of the best books ever written about a journey into the Catholic Church, from perhaps the most famous converts to Catholicism. Dr. Scott Hahn and his wife, Kimberly, lecture around the world, inspiring Catholics to go deeper into their faith.

***Set Your Heart Free (30 Days with a Great Spiritual Teacher, Saint Francis de Sales),* ed. John Kirvan (Notre Dame, IN: Ave Maria Press, 2008).**
Small, daily readings that soothe our stress, calm our anxieties, and build our trust in God. Saint Francis de Sales was a masterful evangelist, and his insights and prayers will bathe your soul in refreshment and peace.

***Diary: Divine Mercy in My Soul,* by Saint Maria Faustina Kowalska (Stockbridge, MA: Marian Press, 2002).**
Who doesn't love Saint Faustina? She brings us the Divine Mercy of Jesus Christ! One of the great Polish saints in the likeness of Saint Maximilian Kolbe and Pope Saint John Paul II, Faustina speaks with clarity and simplicity.

Two titles by Patrick Madrid:
***Surprised by Truth: 11 Converts Give the Biblical and Historical Reasons for Becoming Catholic* (Irving, TX: Basilica Press, 1994); and**
***Surprised by Truth 2: 15 Men and Women Give the Biblical and Historical Reasons for Becoming Catholic* (Bedford, NH: Sophia Institute Press, 2000).**
The *Surprised by Truth* series contains moving stories of people who discovered the truth of the Catholic Church and couldn't help but come home. The books answer common objections to the Catholic Faith and depict in a powerfully personal way the struggles people face on their journey home. These books make great gifts for friends and relatives who are away from the Church.

How to Win the Culture War: A Christian Battle Plan for a Society in Crisis, **by Peter Kreeft (Downers Grove, IL: Intervarsity Press, 2002).**
This book is a masterpiece for today's times, outlining a Christian battle plan for our culture in crisis. If we understand the battle going on in our society — the culture of life versus the culture of death — we are better equipped to join the effort to spread love and truth and win souls back to Christ and his Catholic Church.

Rediscover Catholicism: A Spiritual Guide to Living with Passion and Purpose, **by Matthew Kelly (Cincinnati, OH: Beacon Publishing, 2002).**
Matthew Kelly is one of the most popular Catholic speakers and authors in the world. *Rediscover Catholicism* is a highly recommended book for the New Evangelization!

Wisdom from the Pulpit: A Collection of 80 Short Walks in Everyday Life, **by Rev. George McKenna (Oak Lawn, IL: CMJ Marian Publishers, 2007).**
God bless Father McKenna! Tricia and I met him and discovered this book after Mass at the Midway Airport chapel near Chicago. He served there for years. This is a wonderful collection of inspiring homilies, more profound than most you have ever heard.

Search and Rescue: How to Bring Your Family and Friends into — or Back into — the Catholic Church, **by Patrick Madrid (Bedford, NH: Sophia Institute Press, 2001).**
The title says it all: This book is an excellent go-to resource when it comes to evangelizing the people closest to you and inviting them home to the Catholic Church. Pat Madrid gives concrete, easy-to-follow strategies for starting those often-difficult conversations with loved ones and being God's instrument to call them back to the practice of their Catholic faith.

***Patience: Thoughts on the Patient Endurance of Sorrows
and Sufferings*, by Rev. F. X. Lasance (New York: Benziger
Brothers, 1937).**
A book so tiny, it will fit in the palm of one hand! A great little
companion for your pocket or backpack; for reading everywhere
from short flights to waiting in the carpool lane. In our busy
world, we all need more patience!

***Mere Christianity*, by C. S. Lewis (San Francisco: Harper-
SanFrancisco, 2001).**
One of the most timeless and foundational books in any Chris-
tian's library. Every high school-age student should study the
writings of C. S. Lewis, who is also author of the well-known
Chronicles of Narnia.

***Psalms: A School of Prayer*, by Mark Link, SJ (Chicago:
Thomas More Press, 1996).**
The Psalms bring us into the heart of joy, and more deeply into
contemplative prayer. God loves us, and the Psalms are love
poems from our Creator. Father Link weaves them together into a
wonderful collection of prayers.

***Good News, Bad News: Evangelization, Conversion and the
Crisis of Faith*, by Father C. John McCloskey, III, and Russell Shaw (San Francisco: Ignatius Press, 2007).**
Evangelizing is the responsibility of every Catholic. Father
McCloskey and Russell Shaw, some of the greatest American
evangelizers today, explain how to evangelize with passion and
respect for others, so you can help God change lives in the midst
of our secular culture — one soul at a time.

***John Paul II and the New Evangelization: How You Can
Bring the Good News to Others*, edited by Ralph Martin and
Peter Williamson (Cincinnati, OH: Servant Books, 2006).**
This book is filled with answers to your questions about how to

participate in the New Evangelization, how to evangelize young people, how your parish can get involved in evangelization, and much more. It is a practical and instructional guide to living out Pope Saint John Paul II's call for the New Evangelization.

The Little Way of St. Thérèse of Lisieux: Into the Arms of Love, by John Nelson (Liguori, MO: Liguori Publications, 1998).
Saint Thérèse, the Little Flower, is one of my favorites! She is a Doctor of the Church whose prime charism is simplifying the most direct route to union with God. Her teachings are easy to understand and apply. Saint Thérèse is like no other saint, and she will likely become one of your favorite saints, too.

Father Elijah: An Apocalypse, by Michael O'Brien (San Francisco: Ignatius Press, 1997).
This may be the only fictional novel on my list. Michael O'Brien is a gifted Catholic storyteller. His incredible writing style motivated me to read this 600-some-odd-page masterpiece in a mere four days! *Father Elijah* is a page-turner, filled with the realism of spiritual warfare in our day and age. Everyone to whom I've given this recommendation loves this book.

The Emerging Laity: Vocation, Mission, and Spirituality, by Aurelie Hagstrom (Mahwah, NJ: Paulist Press, 2010).
Dr. Hagstrom is a professor of theology at Providence College who lectures on the laity, as well as the gift of welcoming souls home to the Church.

The Interior Castle, by Saint Teresa of Ávila, in *The Collected Works of St. Teresa of Ávila*, vol. 2, trans. Kieran Kavanaugh and Otilio Rodriguez (Washington, DC: ICS Publications, 1980).
The foundress of the Discalced Carmelites and Doctor of the Church, Saint Teresa of Ávila brings us deeper into the spiritual

life and closer to the heart of Christ. Teresa's works, like those of her compatriot Saint John of the Cross, are filled with richness and depth. This book can help strengthen your inner life.

***Whispers from the Cross: Reclaiming the Church Through Personal Holiness*, by Anne, a Lay Apostle (Oak Lawn, IL: CMJ Marian Publishers, 2011).**
Whispers from the Cross seems to touch my soul. After I read a book like this, I say, "I felt like God was personally speaking to me!"

***The Better Part: A Christ Centered Resource for Personal Prayer*, by Father John Bartunek (Modesto, CA: Catholic Spiritual Direction, 2011).**
Mary has chosen the better part, as Scripture teaches. Father Bartunek shares incredible wisdom and spiritual direction with his readers, relating to contemplative prayer and spiritual growth. This is deep reading, filled with pearls.

***The Art of Dying Well (or, How to Be a Saint, Now and Forever)*, by Saint Robert Bellarmine (Bedford, NH: Sophia Institute Press, 2005).**
Our goal is to be saints, and we have a manual — a road map, of sorts — by an expert, a saint himself, to guide us to holiness.

***The Temperament God Gave You: The Classic Key to Knowing Yourself, Getting Along with Others, and Growing Closer to the Lord*, by Art and Laraine Bennett (Bedford, NH: Sophia Institute Press, 2005).**
After reading this book, and many of these authors' other great books, I realized that I am not crazy; I'm just wired in a unique way. Each of us has been programmed by God with a unique personality type, style, and energy level. What appeals to some may not appeal to others. Why? Because each of us is prewired with a certain personality type and temperament to fulfill the

unique mission given to us by God himself! This is an amazing book, and the Bennetts are gifted at knowing our human wiring and how this relates to our spiritual life.

HOLY WISDOM

"For if I preach the gospel, that gives me no ground for boasting. For necessity is laid upon me. Woe to me if I do not preach the gospel!"

(1 CORINTHIANS 9:16)

Evangelization is *"Urgent and Necessary."*

POPE EMERITUS BENEDICT XVI
(Address to the participants at the annual meeting
of the Pontifical Mission Society, May 17, 2008)

"The question confronting the Church today is not any longer whether the man in the street can grasp a religious message, but how to employ the communications media so as to let him have the full impact of the Gospel message."

POPE SAINT JOHN PAUL II
(*International Herald Tribune* [Paris], May 8, 1989)

"The Church is missionary by nature and her principal task is evangelization, which aims to proclaim and to witness to Christ and to promote his Gospel of peace and love in every environment and culture."

POPE EMERITUS BENEDICT XVI
(Address to the participants in the Fifth Annual Congress
of Military Ordinariates, October 26, 2000)

"Evangelizing is in fact the grace and vocation proper to the Church, her deepest identity."

POPE SAINT PAUL VI
(*Evangelii Nuntiandi*, apostolic exhortation, December 8, 1975)

"First let a little love find entrance into their hearts, and the rest will follow."

SAINT PHILIP NERI
("Oratory of St. Philip Neri," by H. Bowden, transcribed by Michael C. Tinkler, from the Catholic Encyclopedia, copyright © 1913 by the Encyclopedia Press, Inc.; electronic version copyright © 1996 by New Advent, Inc.)

"Pray as though everything depended on God. Work as though everything depended on you."

SAINT IGNATIUS OF LOYOLA
(Joseph de Guibert, SJ, *The Jesuits: Their Spiritual Doctrine and Practice* [Chicago: Loyola University Press, 1964], 148.)

"The nation doesn't simply need what we have. It needs what we are."

SAINT TERESA BENEDICTA OF THE CROSS
(also known as Edith Stein) (*Catholic Exchange*, June 6, 2012)

"Christ said, 'I am the Truth'; he did not say, 'I am the custom.'"

SAINT TORIBIO
(from Rev. Alban Butler, *The Lives of the Fathers, Martyrs, and Other Principal Saints*, vol. 3 [New York: D. & J. Sadlier & Co., 1864].)

"As the family goes, so goes the nation, and so goes the whole world in which we live."

POPE SAINT JOHN PAUL II
(Homily at Perth, Australia, November 30, 1986)

POWERFUL PRAYERS

Memorare

Remember, O most gracious Virgin Mary, that never was it
known that anyone who fled to thy protection, implored thy
help, or sought thine intercession was left unaided. Inspired by
this confidence, I fly unto thee, O Virgin of virgins, my Mother;
to thee do I come; before thee I stand, sinful and sorrowful. O
Mother of the Word Incarnate, despise not my petitions, but in
thy mercy hear and answer me. Amen.

Hail Holy Queen

Hail, holy Queen, Mother of mercy!
Hail, our life, our sweetness, and our hope!
To thee do we cry, poor banished children of Eve;
to thee do we send up our sighs, mourning and weeping in this
valley of tears.
Turn, then, most gracious Advocate, thine eyes of mercy toward
us;
and after this our exile show unto us the blessed fruit of thy
womb, Jesus.
O clement, O loving, O sweet Virgin Mary.
Pray for us, O holy mother of God, that we may be made worthy
of the promises of Christ.
Amen.

The Guardian Angel Prayer

Angel of God, my guardian dear, to whom God's love commits
me here, ever this day [night] be at my side, to light and guard, to
rule and guide. Amen.

Prayer to Saint Monica

Exemplary Mother of the great Augustine, you perseveringly pursued your wayward son, not with wild threats but with prayerful cries to heaven.

Intercede for all mothers in our day so that they may learn to draw their children to God. Teach them how to remain close to their children, even the prodigal sons and daughters who have sadly gone astray. Amen.

O glorious St. Monica, greatly challenged among mothers, I feel particularly attracted by you who gave such an enlightened example of motherly love.

Who could understand better than you the anxieties and fears of a mother worrying about the eternal salvation of her children? You endured all, since in the order of nature, St. Augustine is the fruit of your womb, and in the order of grace, the fruit of your tears. For this reason I am greatly convinced that if you here on earth, with the sanctity of your life and the perseverance of your prayers, were one of the great models of the Christian mother, you must enjoy in heaven the privilege of being their singular protector.

Obtain for me the grace to faithfully imitate your virtues, and furthermore, may my children avoid those errors and failures you disapproved of so strongly in your son. And if it will happen, to my misfortune, that they too fall, grant me the grace to obtain with my prayers, supported by yours, as perfect a conversion as you were able to obtain for your son. Amen.

Prayer to Saint Michael

Saint Michael the Archangel,
defend us in battle;
be our protection against the wickedness and snares of the devil.
May God rebuke him, we humbly pray,
and do thou, O Prince of the heavenly host,
by the power of God,

thrust into hell Satan and all the evil spirits
who prowl about the world seeking the ruin of souls.
Amen.

_____

Prayer of Saint Francis of Assisi

Lord, make me an instrument of your peace.
Where there is hatred, let me sow love;
where there is injury, pardon;
where there is doubt, faith;
where there is despair, hope;
where there is darkness, light;
and where there is sadness, joy.
O Divine Master, grant that I may not so much seek
to be consoled as to console;
to be understood as to understand;
to be loved as to love.
For it is in giving that we receive;
it is in pardoning that we are pardoned;
and it is in dying that we are born to eternal life. Amen.

_____

Prayer to Saint Joseph

O St. Joseph, whose protection is so great, so strong, so prompt
before the throne of God, I place in you all my interests and
desires. O St. Joseph, do assist me by your powerful intercession,
and obtain for me from your Divine Son all spiritual blessings
through Jesus Christ, our Lord; so that, having engaged here
below your heavenly power, I may offer my thanksgiving and
homage to the most loving of Fathers.

O St. Joseph, I never weary of contemplating you and Jesus
asleep in your arms. I dare not approach while he reposes near
your heart. Press him in my name and kiss his fine head for me,
and ask him to return the kiss when I draw my dying breath. St.
Joseph, patron of departing souls, pray for me. Amen.

Prayer to the Holy Spirit
(Attributed to Saint Catherine of Siena)
Holy Spirit, come into my heart; draw it to Thee by Thy power,
O my God, and grant me charity with filial fear. Preserve me, O
ineffable Love, from every evil thought; warm me, inflame me
with Thy dear love, and every pain will seem light to me. My Father, my sweet Lord, help me in all my actions. Jesus, love, Jesus,
love. Amen.

Prayer for the Gifts of the Holy Spirit
(Saint Alphonsus Liguori)
Holy Spirit, divine Consoler, I adore You as my true God, with
God the Father and God the Son. I adore You and unite myself to
the adoration You receive from the angels and saints.

I give You my heart, and I offer my ardent thanksgiving for
all the grace which You never cease to bestow on me.

O Giver of all supernatural gifts, who filled the soul of the
Blessed Virgin Mary, Mother of God, with such immense favors,
I beg You to visit me with Your grace and Your love and to grant
me the gift of holy fear, so that it may act on me as a check to
prevent me from falling back into my past sins, for which I beg
pardon.

Grant me the gift of piety, so that I may serve You for the
future with increased fervor, follow with more promptness Your
holy inspirations, and observe your divine precepts with greater
fidelity.

Grant me the gift of knowledge, so that I may know the
things of God and, enlightened by Your holy teaching, may walk,
without deviation, in the path of eternal salvation.

Grant me the gift of fortitude, so that I may overcome courageously all the assaults of the devil, and all the dangers of this
world which threaten the salvation of my soul.

Grant me the gift of counsel, so that I may choose what is
more conducive to my spiritual advancement and may discover

the wiles and snares of the tempter.

Grant me the gift of understanding, so that I may apprehend the divine mysteries and by contemplation of heavenly things detach my thoughts and affections from the vain things of this miserable world.

Grant me the gift of wisdom, so that I may rightly direct all my actions, referring them to God as my last end; so that, having loved him and served him in this life, I may have the happiness of possessing him eternally in the next. Amen.

Come Holy Spirit

Come Holy Spirit, fill the hearts of Thy faithful and kindle in them the fire of Thy love.

V. Send forth Thy Spirit, and they shall be created;

R. And Thou shalt renew the face of the earth.

Let us pray.

O, God, who by the light of the Holy Spirit, did instruct the hearts of the faithful, grant that by the same Holy Spirit we may be truly wise and ever rejoice in His consolations. Through Christ our Lord. Amen.

Invocation to the Sacred Heart
(Saint Margaret Mary Alacoque)

O Heart of love, I put all my trust in Thee; for I fear all things from my own weakness, but I hope for all things from Thy goodness. Amen.

For the Help of the Sacred Heart

Take away, O my Jesus, the blindness of my heart, that I may know Thee; take away the hardness of my heart, that I may fear Thee; take away the coldness of my heart, that I may resist everything that is contrary to Thy will; take away its heavy, earthly

sluggishness and selfishness, that I may be capable of heroic sacrifice for Thy glory, and for the souls whom Thou has redeemed
with Thy own most precious blood. Amen.

Prayer by Blessed John Henry Cardinal Newman,
Prayed by Blessed Mother Teresa's Sisters of Charity.
Dear Jesus, help me to spread Your fragrance everywhere I go.
Flood my soul with Your spirit and life.
Penetrate and possess my whole being so utterly
that my life may only be a radiance of Yours.
Shine through me and be so in me
that every soul I come in contact with
may feel Your presence in my soul.
Let them look up and see no longer me, but only Jesus!
Stay with me and then I shall begin to shine as You shine,
so to shine as to be a light to others.
The light, O Jesus, will be all from You; none of it will be mine;
it will be you, shining on others through me.
Let me thus praise you in the way which you love best,
by shining on those around me.
Let me preach you without preaching, not by words but by my
example,
by the catching force, the sympathetic influence of what I do,
the evident fullness of the love my heart bears for you. Amen.

For the Peace of Christ
(Blessed John Henry Cardinal Newman)
O most sacred, most loving heart of Jesus, Thou art concealed in
the Holy Eucharist, and Thou beatest for us still. Now as then
Thou sayest, "With desire I have desired." I worship Thee, then,
with all my best love and awe, with my fervent affection, with my
most subdued, most resolved will. O make my heart beat with
Thy heart. Purify it of all that is earthly, all that is proud and

sensual, all that is hard and cruel, of all perversity, of all disorder, of all deadness. So fill it with Thee, that neither the events of the day nor the circumstances of the time may have power to ruffle it; but that in Thy love and Thy fear it may have peace.

The shortest, simplest, and most powerful prayer: the name of Jesus.

Catholic Organizations

I haven't traveled along my faith journey alone. Here's a list of great Catholic organizations that have blessed my life, as well as the lives of many others. Check them out:

Catholic Radio Association
A trade association for Catholic radio stations, www.catholicradioassociation.org

Eternal Word Television Network (EWTN)
A Catholic television and radio network and website, www.ewtn.com

The Integrated Catholic Life
An e-magazine about integrating faith, family, and world, www.integratedcatholiclife.org

Knights of Columbus
A Catholic fraternal benefits organization, www.kofc.org

Knights of the Holy Sepulcher
The only lay institute of the Vatican State charged with providing for the needs of the Latin Patriarchate of Jerusalem; its members fund activities that support the Christian presence in the Holy Land, www.holysepulchre.net

Legatus
An organization of practicing Catholic lay men and women
(along with their spouses) who are CEOs, presidents, managing
partners, and business owners who live and share the Catholic
Faith in every area of their lives, www.legatus.org

Marian Conference
An organization that hosts conferences across the United States,
promoting devotion to our Blessed Mother and helping participants grow closer to Christ, www.marianconference.org

Opus Dei
A personal prelature whose members strive to turn work and daily
activities into occasions for growing closer to God, serving others,
and improving society, www.opusdei.org

Order of Malta
An organization whose members make a commitment to achieve
spiritual perfection while serving the poor and the sick, www.
orderofmalta.int

Regnum Christi
An apostolic movement made up of laypeople, deacons, and
priests who share the charism of the Legionaries of Christ, www.
regnumchristi.org

About the Author

Following twenty-five years as an award-winning corporate advertising executive, Tom Peterson's life would radically change after receiving a transforming spiritual conversion while on a Catholic retreat. Soon afterward, he founded three media apostolates: *virtuemedia.org* (pro-life), *catholicscomehome.org* (New Evangelization), and *amenalleluia.org*.

With God's grace, Catholics Come Home was the first faith group ever to air on national networks like CBS, NBC, and ESPN, and has reached more than three hundred million viewers since 1998, helping more than a half-million souls home to Jesus and his Catholic Church! The website is featured globally in nine languages.

Tom hosts a popular prime-time television series called *Catholics Come Home*, in its sixth season worldwide on EWTN, airing Sunday and Monday evenings.

Tom has presented internationally at more than five hundred Catholic conferences, including at the Vatican, had multiple appearances on national media outlets, and has authored five popular books. Tom has been a member of Legatus International for eighteen years, and served as vice chairman.

Tom and his wife, Tricia, have been married for more than thirty-four years and have three daughters, two sons-in-law, and seven grandchildren.